Stop Doing Stupid S#*%!

Andreas Wieman and Tim Keefe

Contributors:
Anne Stephanie Cruz, Marina Tiopisto,
Aiza King, Nanditha Nagaraj,
Jennifer Valencia, Jemmarie Bocalbos

FOREWORD

In the often bewildering world of business, there's a universal truth that many of us have learned the hard way: sometimes, we just need to "Stop Doing Stupid S#*%!." It's a phrase that might make you chuckle, but its wisdom runs deep. In the complex realm of modern organizations, where people, processes, and technology intersect, this candid and humorous book offers a refreshing take on how to thrive while avoiding the pitfalls of, well, stupid decisions.

"Stop Doing Stupid S#*%!" is not your typical business guide. It's not stuffy or overly serious. Instead, it's a lively and entertaining exploration of best practices in managing people, processes, and technology, all while keeping a keen eye on the often-neglected aspects of customer and employee experiences. With wit and humor, this book provides valuable insights that are as practical as they are entertaining.

As a professional with experience both inside businesses and as a consultant, I've seen it all—brilliant strategies thwarted by self-sabotage, promising initiatives derailed by senseless missteps, and teams bogged down in bureaucratic nonsense. What sets this book apart is its unapologetic honesty in addressing these issues head-on. Through relatable anecdotes and sharp humor, Tim and Andreas illuminate the pitfalls that can undermine even the most well-intentioned endeavors.

When it comes to people, this book takes a lighthearted yet astute approach to the art of leadership. It recognizes that people are wonderfully complex creatures, and managing them effectively requires not only logic but empathy, humor, and a healthy dose of humility. You'll learn how to foster a culture that celebrates diversity, encourages creativity, and values the well-being of your most important asset—your people.

On processes you'll discover how to make your organization's processes work for you, not against you. The authors reveal how to tackle bureaucracy, eliminate unnecessary red tape, and embrace change without causing chaos. They do so with a dose of humor that reminds us that sometimes, the best way to improve a process is to cut through the nonsense and simply stop doing what doesn't make sense.

Tim and Andreas explores the wild world of digital transformation, data, and technological innovation. With wit and wisdom, you'll gain insights into how to navigate the ever-evolving landscape of technology while avoiding costly mistakes. It's a reminder that technology is a tool, not a solution in itself, and that successful integration requires a thoughtful and strategic approach.

And finally, throughout the book, you'll find a thread of irreverent humor that highlights the critical importance of customer and employee experiences. The authors recognize that happy employees make for happy customers, and they demonstrate how to create an organizational culture that not only avoids "stupid shit" but actively nurtures the well-being of all involved.

In a world where business books can sometimes be overly dry and laden with jargon, "Stop Doing Stupid S#*%T" stands out as a refreshing and enjoyable read that delivers real-world insights with a side of laughter. It's a reminder that while the business world can be serious, it doesn't always have to take itself so seriously.

So, whether you're a seasoned executive, a budding entrepreneur, or just someone looking for a good laugh while learning a thing or two about business, this book is for you. It's a guide to not only stopping the stupid shit but having a blast while doing it.

Here's to a smarter, funnier, and more successful journey in business!

Warmest regards,
Marina Tiopisto

TABLE OF CONTENTS

INTRODUCTION

Introducing "Stop Doing Stupid S#*%!" – a groundbreaking guide meticulously designed to transform how you navigate your daily challenges. In a world where time is a precious commodity, this guide is your ultimate ally, meticulously crafted to align with the pace of modern life. Gone are the days of wading through dense chapters; here, you'll find a revolutionary structure that mirrors the demands of your reality – fast, practical, and effective.

Bursting with streamlined strategies, "Stop Doing Stupid S#*%!" dismantles the traditional barriers to knowledge consumption. No more slogging through endless paragraphs; each chapter is a compact powerhouse, laser-focused on delivering actionable insights. Every technique and concept is tailored to the urgency of today's world, allowing you to learn, apply, and conquer in record time.

With quick reference summaries at the end of each chapter, you can swiftly recap key takeaways and dive straight into implementation. Our goal is not just to inform but to empower – to equip you with the tools you need to excel in real-time scenarios. Whether it's time management, decision-making, communication, or problem-solving, each page is a direct pathway to mastery.

"Stop Doing Stupid S#*%!" is more than a book; it's a dynamic companion on your journey to optimization. Be ready to absorb knowledge like never before, revolutionizing your approach to daily tasks. Get ready to embrace a new era of efficiency and practicality – because success belongs to those who act swiftly and strategically in today's world.

Section 1

Complexity, Made Simple

Complexity, that wonderfully straightforward and easy-to-grasp concept! Who doesn't wake up every morning with an insatiable thirst for understanding complex systems? If you're one of those rare individuals who finds joy in deciphering intricate puzzles, then welcome to "Complexity, Explained Simply" – a journey into the depths of, well, let's call it "simplicity."

Now, you might be wondering why we're bothering to explain complexity in a simple manner. After all, it's not like complex things are, well, complex or anything. But fear not, dear reader, because we're about to break down complexity into tiny, bite-sized pieces, just like your grandma's secret apple pie recipe. And don't worry, it's not like you need a PhD in quantum physics, a dictionary of obscure terms, and a gallon of coffee to understand it. Or do you?

So, grab your intellectual snorkel because we're about to dive into the murky waters of complexity theory. In this place, simple becomes complicated, and complicated becomes... well, let's just say you might reconsider your life choices. But hey, if you're here, you're either a glutton for punishment or a true seeker of knowledge. Either way, prepare to be amazed, befuddled, and hopefully entertained as we attempt to make complexity look as simple as rocket science!

***

Complex models and strategies have become the norm in the ever-evolving business landscape. While these intricate frameworks are designed to drive growth and success, they often present a significant challenge: they can be overwhelmingly convoluted for the average employee. However, there's a compelling case for simplifying and explaining these complex business models in simple terms.

This transformative approach not only empowers employees with a clearer understanding of their organization's intricacies but also profoundly enhances their contributions and productivity. In this exploration, we will explore why translating complexity into simplicity is a powerful strategy for unlocking the untapped potential of a workforce and driving sustainable success within an organization.

Transforming complex business models into non-specific, easier-to-understand simulations and training programs can profoundly impact an organization by fostering a culture of education and data-driven decision-making. Simplified simulations break down intricate concepts, making them accessible to a broader audience within the company.

This democratization of knowledge ensures that all employees, regardless of their background or role, can grasp essential business dynamics. Interactive simulations engage employees in hands-on learning, allowing them to experiment with different scenarios and apply theoretical knowledge to real-world situations. They become better equipped to make data-driven decisions in their roles as they gain confidence and proficiency through progressive learning paths and customized training tracks. By integrating real company data and promoting regular assessments, these programs bridge the gap between theory and practice.

Additionally, encouraging peer collaboration and leadership participation creates a sense of collective learning and accountability. Over time, this approach equips employees with the skills needed for informed decision-making and cultivates a cultural shift where data-driven insights become integral to the organization's DNA.

CHAPTER 1: GETTING STARTED

Explaining complex business concepts to entry-level employees can be challenging, but here are some practical tips to make it easier and more understandable for them:
Use Plain Language

Avoid using jargon and technical terms that may confuse entry-level employees. Instead, use simple and concise language to explain concepts. Break down complex terms into relatable examples or everyday analogies. Here's how:

- Clarity and Comprehension: Plain language simplifies complex jargon and technical terms, allowing employees to understand critical business concepts more quickly. When employees grasp the fundamentals, they can build upon this knowledge, leading to more informed decision-making and creative problem-solving.

- Reducing Miscommunication: Complex business language often leads to miscommunication and misunderstandings. When employees are on the same page, they can communicate more effectively and collaborate to find innovative solutions to business challenges.

- Empowering Diverse Teams: Organizations today often have diverse workforces with varying expertise and backgrounds. Using plain language ensures that everyone, regardless of their prior knowledge or experience, can participate in discussions, contribute ideas, and propose solutions.

- Breaking Down Silos: Complex language can create silos within organizations, where different departments struggle to understand each other's objectives and challenges. Plain language breaks down these barriers, fostering cross-functional collaboration and sharing fresh perspectives to address complex issues.

- Encouraging Questions: Employees are more likely to feel comfortable asking questions when information is presented in plain language. This curiosity can lead to deeper exploration and innovative problem-solving as individuals seek to understand the "why" and "how" behind business processes.

- Streamlining Training and Onboarding: Plain language is especially beneficial for new hires and those undergoing training. It accelerates their learning curve, allowing them to become productive team members faster and contribute innovative ideas sooner.

- Enhancing Customer-Centricity: Simplifying complex business concepts can also extend to customer-facing interactions. When employees can explain products, services, and solutions in plain language, they create a more positive customer experience and may uncover innovative ways to meet customer needs.

- Promoting a Culture of Innovation: When employees are unburdened by complex language and can easily grasp business concepts, they are more likely to think creatively and propose innovative solutions to challenges. This cultural shift toward innovation can lead to continuous improvement and competitive advantages.

- Agility in Problem-Solving: Plain language enables agile problem-solving. When employees can quickly understand the nuances of a problem, they can adapt and pivot more efficiently, responding to changing market conditions and customer demands.

Adopting plain language in business communication empowers employees with the knowledge and understanding to tackle complex challenges creatively and collaboratively. It bridges gaps, encourages questions, and promotes a culture where innovative problem-solving becomes the norm, driving business growth and adaptability in an increasingly competitive world.

Start with the Big Picture

Using the big-picture approach is a powerful strategy for making complex business topics more accessible, relatable, and conducive to innovative problem-solving for employees. When employees have a clear grasp of the organization's overarching goals, objectives, and strategies, they can better contextualize complex details and see how their work contributes to the larger mission. This holistic perspective helps them understand what they need to do and why it matters.

By connecting their roles to the broader business context, employees are more motivated and engaged, as they can see the impact of their contributions.

Moreover, employees with a big-picture view are more likely to find innovative solutions when facing complex challenges. They can draw on their understanding of the organization's goals to identify opportunities, anticipate potential roadblocks, and propose creative ideas that align with the overall strategy.

This approach enhances problem-solving and fosters a culture of collaboration and alignment where employees work collectively toward shared objectives, ultimately driving organizational success. This context can make complex concepts more relatable and meaningful.

Visualizing Information is a Powerful Tool

Visualize information for conveying complex ideas simply and understandably. Whether you're presenting data, explaining a concept, or trying to engage your audience, visual aids such as charts, diagrams, and infographics can significantly enhance your communication. This guide will show you how to effectively utilize visual aids to simplify complex information and make it more engaging, memorable & easier to understand and remember.

• Understand Your Audience:
Before creating visual aids, consider your target audience's background, knowledge level, and preferences. Tailor your visuals to match their needs and expectations, ensuring your message effectively resonates with them.

• Choose the Right Visual Representation:
Selecting the appropriate visual representation is crucial. Different types of information are best conveyed through specific visual aids:

1. Charts and Graphs: Use bar charts, line graphs, pie charts, and scatter plots for numerical data comparisons and trends.

2. Diagrams: Employ flowcharts, process diagrams, and mind maps to illustrate processes, relationships, and hierarchies.

3. Infographics: Create infographics to combine text, images, and icons to provide a comprehensive overview of complex topics.

• Keep it Simple:
Simplicity is key when visualizing information. Avoid clutter and complexity; instead, focus on clarity and concise representation. Use a limited color palette and clear fonts to ensure readability.

• Highlight Key Information:
Emphasize the most critical points or data by using contrasting colors, bold fonts, or annotations. This helps your audience quickly grasp the essential takeaways.

• Label and Title Carefully:
Ensure that all elements in your visual aids are appropriately labeled and have a clear title or heading. Labels and titles provide context and guide the viewer through the information.

• Provide Context:
Include brief explanations or captions to help your audience understand the significance of the visual aid. Contextual information provides clarity and prevents misinterpretation.

• Use Consistency:
Maintain consistency in your visual aids. If you use specific symbols, colors, or styles for particular elements, stick to them throughout your presentation. Consistency helps with understanding and reduces confusion.

• Test for Comprehension:
Before using your visual aids in a presentation or publication, test them with a small audience to ensure they effectively convey your message and are easy to understand.

• Adapt to Different Mediums:
Consider the platform or medium through which your visual aids will be shared. Optimize them for print, web, or presentations to ensure they maintain their effectiveness.

• Keep Accessibility in Mind:
Ensure your visual aids are accessible to all audiences, including those with disabilities. Use alt text for images and follow accessibility guidelines for color choices and fonts.

Visualizing information through charts, diagrams, and infographics is valuable for simplifying complex ideas and making them more accessible. By understanding your audience, choosing the right visual representation, and following best practices, you can effectively communicate information and leave a lasting impact on your audience.

Make it Relatable

Understanding complex concepts is essential for informed decision-making and problem-solving. To help employees grasp these concepts more effectively, bridging the gap between theory and practical application is crucial. This guide will show you how to relate complex ideas to real-world examples within the business context.

• Understand Your Audience:
Start by understanding your employees' backgrounds, knowledge levels, and experiences. This insight will help you choose relevant real-world examples that resonate with them.

• Identify Key Concepts:
Clearly define the complex concepts you want to explain. Break them down into smaller, digestible parts. This will make it easier to connect them to real-world scenarios.

11

- Choose Familiar Situations: Look for everyday situations or common business scenarios that align with the complex concepts. Employees are more likely to relate to examples they encounter in their work or personal lives.

- Use Analogies: Analogies are powerful tools for simplifying complex concepts. Compare the unfamiliar idea to a familiar one. For example, liken financial risk to investing in stocks, where higher risk can lead to higher returns.

- Tell Stories: Narratives are memorable and engaging. Craft stories illustrating how the concept played out in a business situation. Stories can bring concepts to life and show their impact.

- Show Cause and Effect:Demonstrate the cause-and-effect relationship between the complex concept and its real-world consequences. Use before-and-after scenarios to highlight the concept's importance.

- Encourage Participation:Engage employees by encouraging them to share their real-world experiences related to the concept. This fosters discussion and allows them to connect on a personal level.

- Provide Case Studies:Offer real case studies from your industry or business. Analyze these cases to show how the concepts influenced strategic decisions and outcomes.

- Relate to Goals:Connect complex concepts to the broader organizational goals. Explain how understanding these concepts can contribute to achieving company objectives, making them more relevant to employees.

- Relate to Daily Tasks:Show how employees can apply these concepts to their daily tasks and responsibilities. Offer practical tips and guidelines for implementation.

- Use Feedback: Gather feedback from employees to understand which real-world examples resonated the most. This can help you refine your approach for future training or explanations.

Relating complex concepts to real-world examples is a powerful way to enhance employees' understanding and engagement. By choosing relatable situations, using analogies, telling stories, and providing practical applications, you can help employees see the functional relevance of these concepts within the business context.

This not only aids comprehension but also encourages employees to apply their newfound knowledge effectively in their roles.

Provide Step by Step Views

Complex processes and workflows can be overwhelming, especially for entry-level employees. To foster understanding and empower them to contribute effectively, it's essential to provide step-by-step explanations.

This guide outlines how to break down complex processes into sequential steps, emphasizing cause-and-effect relationships to help entry-level employees comprehend how different components fit together and impact the overall process.

- Define the Process or Workflow:
Start by clearly defining the complex process or workflow you

intend to explain. Provide context and highlight its importance within the organization.

• Break it Down into Sequential Steps:
Identify the discrete steps or phases within the process. Divide the workflow into manageable parts to prevent overwhelming your audience.

• Begin with an Overview:
Before diving into the individual steps, present a high-level overview of the entire process. This provides employees with a roadmap of what to expect.

• Focus on Cause and Effect Relationships:
In each step, explain the cause-and-effect relationships between actions. Describe how completing one step affects the subsequent steps and the overall outcome.

• Use Clear and Concise Language (Plain Language):
Keep your explanations simple and avoid jargon or technical terms that entry-level employees may not understand. Use everyday language to enhance comprehension.

• Provide Visual Aids:
Support your explanations with visual aids like flowcharts, diagrams, or process maps. Visuals can make complex concepts more tangible and easier to follow.

• Highlight Key Milestones:
Identify critical milestones or checkpoints within the process. Explain their significance and how they mark progress.

• Include Examples:
Illustrate each step with practical examples or scenarios. Real-life examples help employees relate the theoretical knowledge to practical situations.

• Encourage Questions and Feedback:
Create an environment where employees feel comfortable asking questions and seeking clarification. Address any queries promptly to ensure clarity.

• Offer Practice Opportunities:
Provide opportunities for employees to practice the steps in a controlled setting. Hands-on experience can reinforce their understanding and build confidence.

• Summarize and Recap:
At the end of each explanation or section, summarize the key points and recap the cause-and-effect relationships. Reinforce what employees have learned.

• Relate to Their Roles:
Help employees connect the process to their specific roles and responsibilities. Explain how their actions contribute to the successful execution of the process.

• Assess Understanding:
Conduct assessments or quizzes to gauge employees' comprehension of the step-by-step explanations. Use their performance to identify areas that may require further clarification.

Providing step-by-step explanations for complex processes or workflows is fundamental to empowering entry-level & tenured employees. By breaking down the process, emphasizing cause-and-effect relationships, using clear language, and offering support through visual aids and examples, you can enhance their understanding and confidence.

This approach not only aids in comprehension but also enables employees to see how their actions impact the organization's overall success.

Encourage Questions and Active Learning

Fostering an open and supportive work environment is essential for nurturing a culture of continuous learning and growth within an organization. By creating such an atmosphere, employees are more likely to feel comfortable asking questions and actively participating in discussions, enhancing their ability to internalize and retain information effectively.

• Promoting Psychological Safety:
A key component of an open and supportive environment is psychological safety. When employees feel secure in expressing their thoughts and asking questions without fear of ridicule or judgment, they are more inclined to engage in active learning. Encouraging an atmosphere where diverse opinions are valued helps individuals feel respected and heard.

• Valuing Curiosity:
An essential aspect of active learning is curiosity. Encourage employees to be curious by demonstrating that asking questions is not a sign of weakness but a pathway to knowledge and growth. Leaders can set an example by asking questions themselves and demonstrating a genuine thirst for knowledge.

• Regular Knowledge Sharing Sessions:
Implement regular knowledge-sharing sessions where employees can discuss their ideas and ask questions. These sessions can take various forms, from team meetings to workshops, but the key is to provide a dedicated space for open dialogue. This practice also promotes cross-functional collaboration and the exchange of expertise.

- Active Listening:

Actively listening to employees' questions and input is crucial. Leaders and colleagues should pay full attention when someone is speaking, show empathy, and respond constructively. This helps employees feel valued and creates a positive feedback loop that encourages further participation.

- Encourage Constructive Feedback:

In an open environment, constructive feedback is invaluable. Encourage employees to provide feedback on processes, projects, and team dynamics. Constructive criticism should be viewed as an opportunity for growth, not a personal attack.

- Recognize and Reward Curiosity:

Acknowledge and reward employees who actively engage in learning and contribute meaningfully to discussions. This recognition can be in the form of promotions, bonuses, or public recognition, as it reinforces the value placed on curiosity and active participation.

- Provide Learning Resources:

Make learning resources readily available to employees. This can include access to books, courses, or online resources that align with their interests and career goals. Encouraging employees to take ownership of their learning journey can lead to more engaged and empowered teams.

- Supportive Leadership:

Leadership plays a pivotal role in creating an environment conducive to active learning. Leaders should encourage questions and discussions and actively participate in them. They should be approachable and willing to mentor and guide employees in their quest for knowledge.

- Feedback Loops:

Establish feedback loops where employees can express their concerns or suggest improvements regarding the learning environment. Use this feedback to continuously refine and enhance the supportive culture.

- Measure and Celebrate Progress:

Set measurable goals for the organization's learning and development initiatives, and celebrate achievements. This creates a sense of accomplishment and motivates employees to continue their active learning journey.

Creating an open and supportive environment where employees feel comfortable asking questions and engaging in discussions is a cornerstone of fostering a culture of continuous learning. Such an environment empowers individuals to actively seek knowledge, share insights, and contribute to the collective growth of the organization, ultimately leading to increased innovation and success.

Offer Training and Development Opportunities

To cultivate a thriving workforce and ensure the long-term success of an organization, it is imperative to offer comprehensive training and development opportunities, especially tailored to entry-level employees. Such initiatives are a vital foundation for their professional growth and contribution to the organization's objectives. By providing structured training sessions, workshops, and accessible online resources, employers can address these employees' specific needs and knowledge levels, ensuring that the learning experience is both engaging and beneficial.

These resources should be meticulously tailored to match the entry-level employees' current understanding, gradually introducing more complex concepts as their expertise and familiarity with the organization's operations evolve. This approach bolsters their confidence and equips them with the skills and knowledge necessary to excel in their roles. Moreover, it conveys a profound commitment to their development, fostering a sense of loyalty and dedication among entry-level employees. In essence, investing in targeted training and development opportunities not only empowers individuals to thrive but also contributes to the overall growth and dynamism of the organization.

Use Stories and Case Studies

Leveraging the power of storytelling and real-life case studies is a remarkably effective strategy for engaging employees and enhancing their understanding of complex business concepts. Leaders can foster a deeper connection between employees and the company's mission by sharing success stories and examples of how the organization navigated challenges and achieved favorable outcomes. Stories, often relatable and emotionally resonant, transcend the confines of data and statistics, making information more memorable and meaningful.

These narratives illustrate the practical application of business strategies and provide valuable context, showcasing how individual actions contribute to collective success. By humanizing the organization's achievements and highlighting the roles played by various team members, employees can see their potential impact within the company. This, in turn, instills a sense of purpose and motivation, as employees are inspired to emulate the behaviors and approaches that led to these successes.

Stories and case studies can elucidate complex concepts by presenting them realistically. Instead of abstract theories, employees can grasp the nuances of business challenges and solutions through relatable examples. This approach promotes a deeper understanding, as employees learn "what" was done and "why" it was effective, fostering critical thinking and problem-solving skills.

In essence, weaving stories and case studies into organizational communication and training initiatives enriches the learning experience by engaging employees on an emotional level and facilitating the internalization of knowledge.
It creates a shared narrative that aligns employees with the company's values and goals, ultimately fostering a more informed, motivated, and cohesive workforce.

 CHAPTER 2: PROVIDE ONGOING SUPPORT

Success Sponsors

Acknowledging that learning is a continuous journey and that all employees may require ongoing support and guidance is fundamental to nurturing their professional growth within an organization. Such sustained support is paramount for their development and integration into the company's operations. Assigning Success Sponsors or experienced colleagues to act as resources and guides is a proactive approach to facilitate this process.

Success Sponsors (Mentors) serve as invaluable assets in the learning process, offering a personalized and empathetic connection for entry-level employees. They can provide immediate answers to questions, share practical insights from their own experiences, and offer advice tailored to employees' specific challenges as they navigate complex business concepts. This Success Sponsorship accelerates the learning curve and instills a sense of camaraderie and belonging, as it signifies the organization's investment in their success.

Moreover, ongoing support acknowledges the dynamic nature of the business landscape, where new challenges and opportunities continually arise. Employees benefit immensely from having a trusted mentor or colleague who can help them adapt to changing circumstances and evolving business strategies. This support system creates a safety net, encouraging employees to explore, learn, and innovate with the confidence that they have a knowledgeable ally to turn to.

Recognizing that learning extends beyond the initial onboarding phase and providing entry-level employees with ongoing support through Success Sponsors or experienced colleagues is a strategic investment in their professional development and overall job satisfaction. It reinforces their sense of belonging within the organization, empowers them to navigate complexity confidently, and ensures they remain agile and adaptable in a constantly evolving business environment. Ultimately, this commitment to ongoing support enhances employee retention and contributes to the organization's long-term success.

The presence of trusted Success Sponsors for entry-level employees within an organization offers substantial benefits to both the organization itself and the Success Sponsors involved:

For the Organization

- Enhanced Employee Retention: When entry-level employees can access Success Sponsors, organizations benefit from higher retention rates. The guidance and support provided by Success Sponsors can help newcomers overcome challenges, adapt to the company culture, and feel more valued, reducing the likelihood of turnover.

- Accelerated Learning and Productivity: With Success Sponsors available to assist entry-level employees, the learning curve is shortened. This means these employees can become productive contributors more quickly, positively impacting the organization's bottom line.

- Knowledge Transfer and Succession Planning: Mentoring facilitates the transfer of knowledge, skills, and best practices within the organization. It helps preserve institutional knowledge and aids succession planning by grooming potential leaders from within the workforce.

- Improved Team Cohesion: Success Sponsorship promotes a culture of collaboration and teamwork. When entry-level employees have Success Sponsors who guide and integrate them into the team, it fosters a more cohesive and harmonious work environment.

- Positive Employer Branding: Organizations that invest in Success Sponsorship programs showcase a commitment to employee development, which can boost their reputation as an employer of choice. This can attract top talent and enhance the company's brand image.

For the Success Sponsors

Professional Development: Serving as a mentor allows experienced employees to develop their leadership, coaching, and interpersonal skills. Mentoring can be a fulfilling and enriching experience that enhances their professional growth.

Increased Job Satisfaction: Success Sponsors often find satisfaction in helping others succeed. This sense of fulfillment can boost their job satisfaction and overall morale, leading to greater job commitment and engagement.

- Enhanced Communication Skills: Mentoring requires effective communication and active listening. As Success Sponsors work with entry-level employees, they improve their communication skills, which can benefit them in various aspects of their work.

- Recognition and Leadership Development: Success Sponsors are typically recognized and valued within the organization for guiding and developing talent. This recognition can lead to increased opportunities for leadership roles and career advancement.

- Personal Reflection and Learning: Success Sponsors may find that mentoring offers them fresh perspectives and insights. By interacting with entry-level employees, Success Sponsors may reflect on their practices and learn new approaches or ideas.

Trusted Success Sponsors benefit both the organization and the Success Sponsors themselves. It enhances the organization's performance, culture, and reputation, while Success Sponsors gain personal and professional satisfaction, improved skills, and potential career advancement opportunities. A Success Sponsorship program can create a win-win situation where everyone involved, including the entry-level employees, thrives and contributes positively to the organization's success.

Modernized Continuing Education

Gamification

Gamification, the application of game elements and mechanics to non-game contexts, can be a powerful tool for fostering a productive and collaborative culture in the workplace, particularly when used for ongoing continuous education. By infusing learning experiences with elements of competition, achievement, and engagement, gamification can motivate employees to actively participate in learning activities, collaborate with their peers, and ultimately contribute to a dynamic and thriving workplace culture.

One of the primary ways gamification promotes a productive culture is by increasing employee engagement. When learning is presented as a game, it becomes inherently more enjoyable and interactive. Employees are more likely to invest time and effort into ongoing education when they find the experience engaging and fun.
This heightened engagement translates into better retention of information, improved problem-solving skills, and a more knowledgeable workforce, all of which contribute to overall productivity.

Gamification encourages a collaborative spirit among employees. Many gamified learning experiences involve teamwork, challenges, or competitions that require individuals to work together to achieve common goals. This collaborative aspect enhances employees' ability to communicate and cooperate and nurtures a sense of camaraderie and shared purpose. Employees who collaborate on solving problems or reaching milestones build stronger relationships, leading to improved teamwork and synergy in their regular work tasks.

Gamification also taps into employees' intrinsic motivation to excel. By earning badges, completing challenges, or climbing leaderboards, employees experience a sense of accomplishment and recognition, which can be highly motivating. This encourages them to actively participate in continuous education and fuels their desire to excel in their daily tasks, leading to increased productivity and a high performance culture.

Furthermore, gamification can provide instant feedback and data on employee progress and performance. This data-driven approach enables managers and HR professionals to identify strengths and weaknesses in employee skills and knowledge, allowing for targeted training and development efforts. This, in turn, supports a culture of continuous improvement, where employees are encouraged to enhance their competencies and contribute more effectively to the organization's success.

Gamification for ongoing, continuous education offers a multifaceted approach to fostering a productive and collaborative workplace culture. By engaging employees, promoting collaboration, tapping into intrinsic motivation, and providing data-driven insights, gamified learning experiences enhance employee skills and contribute to a dynamic and thriving organizational culture where learning, growth, and collaboration are valued and prioritized.

Workshops & Other Online Resources

Workshops and online resources dedicated to ongoing continuous education play a pivotal role in fostering a productive and collaborative workplace culture. These learning opportunities empower employees to continually develop their skills, stay updated on industry trends, and contribute more effectively to the organization's success. Here's how they facilitate a culture of productivity and collaboration:

Firstly, workshops and online resources provide employees with a structured environment for learning. Employees can delve into specific topics or skill sets relevant to their roles by participating in workshops or accessing well-designed online materials. This targeted learning approach enhances their competence and ensures that their efforts are aligned with organizational goals. As employees become more skilled and knowledgeable, they can contribute meaningfully to their teams and projects, increasing productivity.

Furthermore, continuous education opportunities foster a culture of self-improvement and personal accountability. Employees who have access to workshops or online resources are encouraged to take ownership of their learning journey. This mindset shift towards self-directed learning equips them with valuable skills and instills a sense of responsibility for their professional growth. Such an approach promotes a proactive culture where employees are motivated to continuously enhance their abilities and contribute their newfound knowledge to collaborative efforts.

Workshops and online resources also serve as platforms for shared learning experiences. Employees participating in workshops or accessing the same online resources creates a common knowledge base within the organization. This shared understanding can lead to more effective communication and collaboration among team members. Colleagues can reference the same concepts and frameworks, reducing misunderstandings and streamlining decision-making processes. Moreover, the opportunity to discuss and apply what they've learned in a collaborative setting can foster a sense of camaraderie and teamwork.

Additionally, continuous education initiatives, such as workshops and online resources, help break down knowledge silos within an organization. Employees with access to a wide range of learning opportunities are more likely to share their expertise with colleagues. This knowledge sharing enriches the collective knowledge pool and promotes a culture of collaboration and mentorship. Seasoned employees can mentor their peers, and cross-functional teams can draw from diverse skill sets to tackle complex challenges more effectively.

Workshops and online resources dedicated to ongoing continuous education are invaluable tools for cultivating a productive and collaborative workplace culture. They empower employees to develop skills, foster self-improvement and personal accountability, create shared learning experiences, and break down knowledge silos. As a result, organizations that prioritize continuous education initiatives benefit from a more competent workforce and enjoy a culture where productivity and collaboration are celebrated as key drivers of success.

Providing ongoing employee support is not just a wise business strategy; it's also the right thing to do. Recognizing that learning is a continuous journey and offering the necessary resources and guidance demonstrates a commitment to the growth and well-being of your workforce. It nurtures a respect, trust, and reciprocity culture, where employees feel valued and empowered.

Ultimately, by investing in ongoing support, you enhance individual development and contribute to your organization's long-term success and sustainability. It's a testament to your dedication to your employees and your business's overall prosperity.

Balancing Guided Frameworks and Autonomous Decision-Making

Excessive prescription within project management protocols within organizational environments can impede creative ideation, hinder innovative thinking, and curtail overall productivity. It is imperative to avoid undue prescriptiveness to cultivate a conducive work environment.

Several compelling reasons underscore the importance of adopting a more balanced approach:

• Encouragement of Creativity and Innovation:
Granting employees a measure of autonomy and flexibility within their projects stimulates their creative thinking and fosters the emergence of innovative solutions. An environment that permits individuals to explore diverse approaches and ideas is more likely to yield novel problem-solving strategies that might otherwise remain unexplored.

• Cultivation of Ownership and Accountability:
When employees are vested with the authority to make decisions and shape the trajectory of their projects, they develop a deeper sense of ownership and accountability. This heightened responsibility translates into greater motivation and engagement, as employees take pride in their contributions and are more inclined to invest extra effort to achieve excellence.

• Adaptability to Changing Circumstances:
Projects undertaken within large corporations often encounter unforeseen challenges and dynamic shifts in circumstances.

Excessive prescriptiveness can hinder adaptability and hinder the ability to make essential adjustments. Allowing room for flexibility empowers teams to respond to evolving requirements, market fluctuations, and customer feedback, ultimately enhancing the likelihood of successful project outcomes.

• Empowerment and Morale Enhancement:
Empowering employees with the opportunity to contribute their perspectives, make strategic choices, and assume ownership of their work significantly boosts their self-confidence and morale. Such empowerment fosters a constructive workplace culture and elevates overall job satisfaction, increasing retention rates and attracting top-tier talent.

• Augmentation of Efficiency and Productivity:
By avoiding overly rigid frameworks, employees can leverage their expertise and experience to streamline processes and discover efficient pathways to achieve project objectives. Trusting individuals to make decisions rooted in their knowledge base facilitates enhanced work efficiency, thereby reducing superfluous bureaucratic hurdles and operational delays.

• Facilitation of Learning and Professional Growth:
Empowering employees with a degree of autonomy in project execution presents valuable learning and professional development opportunities. When individuals are encouraged to stretch their skill sets, experiment with novel approaches, and learn from successes and setbacks, they acquire new competencies and become more adaptable.

While a degree of guidance and structure remains indispensable within the realm of large-scale projects, achieving the right equilibrium between providing strategic direction and affording flexibility proves pivotal. This approach empowers employees and fuels a culture of creativity and innovation, culminating in superior organizational outcomes.

Unearthing Hidden Talents: The Surprising Strengths of 'Disengaged' Employees

Employees who may seem disengaged on the surface often possess hidden strengths that, when recognized and tapped into, can benefit both the individual and the organization. Here are some of the hidden strengths of disengaged-seeming employees:

- Creativity

Disengaged employees may have the mental space to think outside the box and create creative solutions to problems. They might not conform to the standard way of doing things, which can lead to innovation when their ideas are encouraged and explored.

- Resilience

Some employees appear disengaged because they have learned to cope with challenging situations and workloads. Their ability to endure stress and maintain a level-headed approach can be valuable during crises or high-pressure situations.

- Autonomy

Disengaged employees often prefer working independently and managing their own tasks. They may have a high degree of self-reliance, which can be channeled into roles where autonomy is valued, such as project management or research.

- Observational Skills

Employees who seem disengaged may spend more time observing their surroundings and colleagues. This can lead to a heightened sense of situational awareness, which can be valuable in roles that require a deep understanding of customer behavior, market trends, or internal dynamics.

- Adaptability

Some disengaged-seeming employees are quick to adapt to changes and unpredictable situations. Their apparent indifference may stem from their ability to remain unfazed by disruptions and roll with the punches.

- Empathy

Disengaged employees may appear disconnected from their colleagues, but they might actually possess strong empathetic skills. They can be adept at understanding the emotional needs of others and can be valuable in roles that require a supportive or counseling approach.

- Analytical Thinking

A disengaged appearance could be a result of introspection and analytical thinking. These employees may excel at problem-solving and critical analysis, making them well-suited for roles that involve data analysis or strategic planning.

- Deep Knowledge

Some individuals may seem disengaged because they are deeply immersed in their work or specialized knowledge. Their dedication to a specific area of expertise can be a significant asset in fields that demand niche skills or require in-depth subject matter expertise.

- Conflict Resolution

Disengaged employees might be skilled at managing conflicts by staying neutral and avoiding drama. They can play a crucial role in diffusing tense situations within teams.

- Loyalty

Disengaged-seeming employees may have a strong sense of loyalty to the company, even if it's not outwardly visible. Their commitment can be harnessed through efforts to reconnect with their sense of purpose or by involving them in projects aligned with their values.

Recognizing and tapping into these hidden strengths requires effective management and communication. Leaders should strive to understand their employees' motivations and aspirations and provide opportunities for them to use these strengths to benefit both the individual and the organization.

Building a culture of trust, open communication, and support can go a long way in helping disengaged employees unlock their potential.

Chapter 3: Cultivating an Ideal Employee Workspace

Creating a productive and conducive physical workspace design is crucial for modern organizations to enhance employee well-being, collaboration, creativity, and overall performance.

Essential Elements

• Understand Your Organization's Needs:
Start by understanding your organization's goals, culture, and the specific needs of your workforce. Different industries and teams may require different types of spaces.

• Involve Employees in the Design Process:
Solicit input from employees and involve them in the design process. This ensures the workspace meets their needs and preferences, increasing buy-in and satisfaction.

• Flexible Layouts:
Create a flexible layout that allows for different work styles and tasks. This might include open workstations, private offices, meeting rooms, collaborative spaces, and quiet areas.

- Natural Light and Ventilation:
Maximize natural light and ventilation to create a healthier and more energizing environment. Consider large windows, skylights, and adjustable blinds.

- Ergonomics and Comfort:
Invest in ergonomic furniture and provide comfortable seating. Adjustable desks and chairs can help employees maintain proper posture and reduce discomfort.

- Technology Integration:
To support modern work requirements, ensure the workspace is equipped with the latest technology, including high-speed internet, video conferencing, and collaboration tools.

- Noise Management:
Incorporate noise-absorbing materials, such as acoustic panels and carpeting, to reduce distractions and create a quieter work environment. Designate quiet zones for focused work.

- Color and Aesthetics:
Use color psychology to create a pleasing and motivating atmosphere. Different colors can influence mood and productivity.

- Biophilic Design:
Incorporate elements of nature into the workspace, such as indoor plants, natural materials, and water features. Biophilic design can improve well-being and creativity.

- Breakout Areas:
Design informal breakout areas or lounges where employees can take breaks, socialize, and recharge. These spaces can encourage collaboration and creativity.

- Wellness Spaces:

Consider adding wellness amenities like fitness centers, meditation rooms, or dedicated areas for relaxation and mindfulness.

- Accessibility and Inclusivity:

Ensure that the workspace is accessible to all employees, including those with disabilities. Design with inclusivity in mind, providing spaces that accommodate various needs.

- Energy Efficiency:

Implement energy-efficient lighting and HVAC systems to reduce environmental impact and operating costs.

- Data-Driven Design:

Use data and feedback to continuously evaluate and improve the workspace design. Monitor factors like occupancy rates, temperature, and lighting levels.

- Safety and Health Protocols:

Incorporate safety measures, especially if the workspace is shared during a pandemic or health crisis. This might include spacing out workstations, providing hand sanitizing stations, and improving air filtration.

- Clear Wayfinding:

Ensure employees can easily navigate the workspace with clear signage and wayfinding design.

- Company Branding:

Reflect your company's values and branding through the design, creating a space that reinforces your organization's identity.

- Budget Considerations:
While aiming for an ideal workspace, stay mindful of budget constraints and prioritize essential elements that align with your organization's goals.

- Regular Feedback and Adaptation:
Continuously seek employee feedback and adjust the workspace design as needed to keep it aligned with changing needs.

Creating a productive and conducive physical workspace design is an ongoing process that should evolve as your organization and workforce change. Regularly reviewing and adapting your design ensures that it remains effective and supports your organization's goals.

Unlocking Theta State: The Workspace Enhancement

In the swiftly moving and high-pressure contemporary environment of modern workplaces, achieving peak performance and productivity has become a paramount goal for organizations. Amidst this pursuit, an emerging concept that has gained significant attention is the Theta state of mind. This unique state of consciousness, characterized by deep relaxation and heightened creativity, offers many benefits for individuals and organizations alike. In this introduction, we will explore the Theta state and why organizations need to provide workspaces conducive to helping employees reach this state.

The Theta state represents a state of mind where brainwave activity slows down to a frequency of 4-8 Hertz, typically associated with deep relaxation and a sense of inner calm. This mental state is often experienced just before falling asleep, during meditation, or in moments of deep introspection. What makes the Theta state particularly fascinating is its potential to unlock the door to our subconscious mind, where creative ideas, innovative solutions, and profound insights often reside. In this state, the conscious mind takes a step back, allowing the individual to tap into their inner reservoir of inspiration and creativity.

Now, consider the implications of employees regularly accessing the Theta state within their work environments. The benefits are multifaceted. First and foremost, employees who can reach the Theta state tend to experience reduced stress and anxiety, leading to improved mental health and overall well-being. Such conditions create a fertile ground for enhanced concentration, better decision-making, and increased job satisfaction.

The Theta state has been associated with heightened creativity and problem-solving abilities. During these moments of mental relaxation, novel ideas often emerge, leading to innovative solutions that can drive a company's success and competitiveness. A workforce proficient in reaching the Theta state becomes a valuable asset for organizations striving to stay ahead in a rapidly evolving business landscape.

In light of these advantages, organizations must recognize the importance of providing workspaces that nurture and encourage employees to access the Theta state. These environments should be designed with elements that facilitate relaxation, such as comfortable seating, natural lighting, soothing aesthetics, and quiet spaces for meditation or reflection. Furthermore, cultivating a corporate culture that values mindfulness, encourages regular breaks, and fosters a work-life balance can also create an atmosphere where the Theta state is more readily accessible.

The Theta represents a remarkable mental state with immense potential for personal and professional growth. Organizations that prioritize the creation of workspaces conducive to employees reaching the Theta state stand to gain a workforce that is not only more content and less stressed but also more innovative and creative. In the competitive business world, tapping into the Theta state may just be the key to unlocking a realm of untapped potential and achieving unparalleled success.

Meandering Paths

Providing meandering paths in the office can be beneficial for relaxation and creativity for several reasons:

• Stress Reduction:
Meandering paths, characterized by gentle curves and organic shapes, can mimic the calming effect of natural landscapes. Walking along such paths can reduce stress and promote a sense of relaxation. The absence of sharp angles and rigid lines creates a more soothing and harmonious environment.

• Encouragement of Movement:
Meandering paths encourage employees to move around the office relaxed and unhurriedly. This physical activity can help combat the negative health effects of prolonged sitting and contribute to a more dynamic and active workday. Regular movement can also stimulate creativity by providing mental breaks and changing perspectives.

• Enhanced Creativity:
A meandering path can lead to unexpected encounters and views within the office environment. This can spark creativity by exposing employees to new ideas, people, or perspectives. The winding nature of the path can also symbolize exploration and adventure, stimulating innovative thinking.

• Privacy and Contemplation:
Meandering paths can incorporate secluded nooks or alcoves. These quiet spots can serve as areas for introspection and contemplation, allowing employees to take a break from their tasks and recharge their creativity. The sense of privacy in these spaces can be conducive to deep thinking and problem-solving.

• Natural Elements:
Meandering paths often integrate natural elements like indoor plants, water features, or art installations. These elements are known to have a positive impact on well-being and creativity. The sight, sound, and even scent of these natural features can enhance relaxation and stimulate the imagination.

• Variety and Novelty:
The irregular layout of meandering paths creates a sense of novelty within the office space. Novelty can be inspiring and stimulate creative thinking. Employees are less likely to become mentally fatigued or bored when their environment offers variety and surprises.

• Cognitive Rest:
Meandering paths can provide cognitive rest by offering a change of scenery and pace. This break from focused work can allow the mind to wander, which is often when creative insights and ideas arise. These moments of mental relaxation can lead to innovative thinking.

• Social Interaction:
When meandering paths are strategically designed, they can encourage chance encounters and casual conversations among employees. These interactions can lead to exchanging ideas and perspectives, fostering creativity and collaboration.

- Aesthetic Appeal:

The visual appeal of meandering paths can make the workspace more inviting and enjoyable. Aesthetically pleasing environments tend to positively impact mood and can contribute to relaxation and a more creative mindset.

Incorporating meandering paths into the office design can create a multi-functional space that supports relaxation, movement, social interaction, and creativity. It offers a departure from the traditional, rigid office layout, promoting a more holistic approach to work environments that prioritize employees' well-being and creative potential.

Active Distractions

Engaging in simple activities that free up the mind while keeping the hands busy can be a productive way to boost creativity, reduce stress, and enhance focus. Here are some examples:

- Fidget Toys: Fidget spinners, stress balls, or other tactile fidget toys can keep hands occupied while allowing the mind to wander. These toys can help reduce restlessness and anxiety.

- Coloring Books: Adult coloring books with intricate designs provide a creative outlet and can help relax the mind. Coloring requires concentration but is also a calming activity.

- Doodling: Doodling on a notepad or a whiteboard can be a subconscious way to free up the mind. It allows for creative expression and can lead to innovative thinking.

- Sensory Putty: Putty or clay that can be molded and squeezed can engage the hands while providing a sensory experience. It's a quiet, discreet way to relieve stress and stimulate the mind.

- Rubik's Cube: Solving a Rubik's Cube requires both hands and mental focus. It's a challenging and engaging puzzle that can be a fun way to take a mental break.
- Desk Puzzles: Small puzzles, such as jigsaw puzzles or brain teasers, can be placed on the desk. Solving them quickly can offer a mental break and stimulate problem-solving skills.

- Kaleidoscope or Etch-A-Sketch: These classic toys offer a visual and hands-on experience that can be soothing and mesmerizing. They provide a break from digital screens.

- Knitting or Crocheting: Keeping a knitting or crocheting project at the desk allows employees to work on it during breaks. These activities are repetitive and can have a meditative quality.

- Mini Zen Garden: A miniature Zen garden with sand and small tools can be a calming and grounding activity. Raking patterns in the sand can be a form of mindfulness.

- Hand-Held Puzzles: Hand-held puzzles, such as metal puzzles or wooden brain teasers, can be manipulated to solve different challenges, engaging both hands and the mind.

- Labyrinth or Maze Games: Small labyrinth or maze games that require tilting to navigate a ball through a maze can be captivating and mentally stimulating.

- Origami: Folding paper into intricate shapes and figures can be a quiet and creative way to engage the hands and mind. Origami kits are readily available.

- Building Blocks: Small building blocks like LEGO or magnetic construction sets can be used to create structures and designs, promoting creativity and focus.

- String Art: Pre-made string art kits or DIY projects can be a creative and hands-on way to engage the mind while working with colorful threads.

- Juggling Balls: Learning to juggle with soft balls can be a fun and challenging way to keep hands busy and improve hand-eye coordination.

These activities balance mental engagement and physical movement, offering a break from the typical work tasks while promoting relaxation, creativity, and improved concentration. Cultivating an ideal employee workspace is a journey that involves careful consideration, thoughtful planning, and ongoing commitment. By prioritizing the workspace's physical, psychological, and cultural aspects, you can create an environment where your employees thrive, productivity soars, and job satisfaction surges.

Remember, an ideal workspace is not static; it evolves with the needs and aspirations of your team. So, stay attuned to feedback, adapt to changing circumstances, and continue to invest in your employees' well-being.

Ultimately, by fostering a workspace that inspires creativity, collaboration, and personal growth, you're improving your company's bottom line and creating a fulfilling and enriching experience for everyone involved.

Ctrl + Alt + Play

When strategically integrated and appropriately managed, video games in the workplace can offer a range of substantial benefits to organizations. Far from being mere sources of distraction, video games have emerged as powerful tools that enhance employee performance, collaboration, and overall organizational success. In this context, incorporating video games can foster a more engaging and innovative work environment, improve problem-solving abilities, encourage teamwork and creativity, and even reduce stress among employees. Below we'll explore the diverse ways in which video games can positively impact organizations, transforming them into more dynamic and productive spaces.

• Relaxation and Stress Relief:
Video games provide an enjoyable and immersive way to relax and relieve stress. Engaging gameplay can divert your attention from work-related stressors, helping you unwind and recharge.

Games often involve challenging tasks, which can be mentally engaging without being mentally draining, making them an excellent way to take short breaks and reset your focus.

• Problem Solving and Critical Thinking:
Many video games, particularly puzzle-solving games, require players to think critically and solve complex problems. This can enhance your problem-solving skills and encourage creative thinking.

Games often present players with various challenges, encouraging them to adapt and strategize to overcome obstacles, which can translate into improved decision-making at work.

- Collaboration and Teamwork:
Multiplayer and cooperative video games can foster collaboration and teamwork. They require players to communicate effectively, coordinate actions, and work together to achieve common goals.

These games can improve interpersonal skills, such as communication, cooperation, and conflict resolution, which are valuable for team projects and group tasks in the workplace.
- Time Management and Productivity:
Setting designated gaming breaks can actually improve time management and productivity. Short, structured breaks can help prevent burnout and increase work focus.

Video games can serve as a reward system, motivating employees to complete tasks efficiently with the promise of a gaming break as a reward.

- Skill Development:
Depending on the type of game, employees may develop skills that are transferable to the workplace. For example, strategy games can enhance strategic thinking and planning skills.

Some video games also require precision and quick reflexes, which can improve hand-eye coordination and attention to detail.

- Creativity and Innovation:
Many video games feature immersive and imaginative worlds, which can inspire creativity. Exploring these virtual environments can stimulate your own creative thinking.
Some games encourage players to create their own content, fostering innovation and a sense of accomplishment.

• Mental Engagement and Focus:
Video games demand focused attention, which can help improve your ability to concentrate on tasks at work.

The mental engagement required by games can serve as a mental workout, potentially boosting cognitive abilities over time.

It's important to note that the positive effects of video games in the workplace depend on moderation, individual preferences, and the specific game chosen. Not all games suit the workplace, and excessive gaming can lead to productivity issues. Therefore, both employees and employers need to strike a balance and establish guidelines to ensure that gaming is used as a constructive tool for relaxation and skill development.

Section 2

Compensation and Talent Attraction

Compensation and Talent Attraction, is the whimsical realm where businesses shower their employees with vast fortunes and irresistible perks, all while attracting top-notch talent with the allure of a never-ending carnival of unicorns and rainbows. It's a place where the laws of economics and budget constraints cease to exist, and where every worker gets their own golden goose that lays platinum eggs.

In this whimsical wonderland, companies compete fiercely to outdo each other in a never-ending game of one-upmanship, offering prospective employees not just a job, but a lifetime supply of gourmet chocolates, daily massages from a team of personal masseuses, and the privilege of being serenaded by a live orchestra while they work.

And who can forget the legendary talent attraction techniques? These businesses have cracked the code to summoning the world's most exceptional talent by offering free trips to the moon, 24/7 access to a private jet, and the chance to have lunch with leprechauns who dispense career advice.

Yes, Compensation & Talent Attraction is truly a land of pure fantasy, where reality takes a back seat, and every employee is treated like royalty, as long as they remember to bring their crown and scepter to work (and clock in on time).

***

Ensuring that employees are adequately compensated extends beyond merely offering a competitive salary. It encompasses a holistic approach to their overall well-being, considering factors such as paid time off, support for pursuits that hold personal significance, and cultivating a vibrant and engaging workplace culture. Let's delve deeper into the significance of these elements and explore why they play pivotal roles in employee satisfaction and organizational success. Here are the reasons why each of these factors is important:

Chapter 1: Salary

A fair and competitive salary is crucial for attracting and retaining talented employees. Job satisfaction and motivation increase when employees feel adequately compensated for their skills, expertise, and contributions. It also helps to maintain financial stability and meet personal needs, ensuring employees can focus on their work without undue stress about their financial situation.

Pairing a fair salary to retain and attract talent is crucial for businesses for several reasons:

- Attracting Top Talent: Offering a fair salary ensures that a business can attract high-caliber professionals with the skills and experience necessary to drive the company's success. In competitive job markets, talented individuals are more likely to consider job opportunities with companies that offer competitive compensation packages.

- Reducing Turnover: Employees who feel they are being compensated fairly for their work are likelier to stay with the company for the long term. High turnover can be costly for businesses regarding recruitment, training, and lost productivity. A fair salary helps mitigate this risk by promoting employee loyalty.

- Enhancing Employee Satisfaction: Fair compensation contributes to employee satisfaction and morale. Workers who believe they are paid fairly for their contributions tend to be more engaged, motivated, and committed to their roles. This, in turn, leads to higher productivity and better job performance.

- Attracting Diverse Talent: A fair salary can also help attract a more diverse talent pool. When compensation is equitable, it sends a message that the company values diversity and is committed to providing equal opportunities for all employees, regardless of their background.

- Improving Employer Brand: Companies known for offering fair compensation packages tend to have a stronger employer brand. A positive reputation in this regard can make it easier to attract top talent, as job seekers are more likely to apply to organizations that are seen as fair and ethical employers.

- Competitive Advantage: In competitive industries, businesses with a reputation for fair compensation may have an advantage over rivals that offer less attractive salary packages. This can lead to a stronger workforce and a competitive edge in the marketplace.

- Enhancing Employee Loyalty and Commitment: Fair salaries are a fundamental way to show employees that their contributions are valued. When employees feel valued, they are more likely to be loyal to the company and committed to its goals. This can lead to increased job satisfaction and reduced absenteeism.

- Minimizing Legal Risks: Offering fair compensation helps businesses avoid legal issues related to wage discrimination and unequal pay. Failure to provide equitable pay can result in costly lawsuits and damage a company's reputation.

- Retaining Institutional Knowledge: Employees who are satisfied with their salaries and feel secure in their positions are more likely to stay with the company for the long term. This helps retain valuable institutional knowledge and experience within the organization.

- Fostering a Positive Work Culture: Fair compensation is critical to a positive work culture. When employees perceive fairness in salary structures, it fosters a sense of trust and collaboration among team members, which can lead to a more harmonious and productive work environment.

Pairing a fair salary with talent retention and attraction strategies is essential for businesses looking to build a strong and sustainable workforce. It helps attract and retain top talent and contributes to a positive workplace culture and overall business success.

Chapter 2: Paid time off (PTO)

In the fast-paced world of modern work, where productivity often takes center stage, it's easy to overlook the significance of paid time off (PTO). However, offering sufficient PTO, which includes not only vacation days, sick leave, and personal days, but also performance-based time off, plays a pivotal role in nurturing a thriving and balanced workforce.

PTO is more than just a benefit; it's a fundamental component of employee well-being. It serves as a lifeline that enables employees to rest, recharge, and maintain a healthy work-life balance. This crucial aspect of compensation helps prevent burnout. It enhances mental health, promotes overall employee satisfaction, and sends a powerful message that the organization values its employees' personal lives and recognizes the importance of self-care.

In this exploration of paid time off, we will delve into the myriad ways in which PTO contributes to a more fulfilled and productive workforce, benefitting both employees and their employers alike.

- Recognition and Incentive: This approach acknowledges and rewards employees for their hard work and contributions to the company. Employees who feel that their efforts are recognized and appreciated are more likely to be motivated and engaged in their roles.

- PerformanceLinked Rewards: Linking additional PTO to business contributions and productivity encourages employees to excel. Knowing that their efforts can lead to more time off provides a tangible incentive to perform at their best, boosting overall productivity and performance.

- WorkLife Balance: Employees highly value PTO as it allows them to recharge, relax, spend quality time with their families, and pursue personal interests. Offering additional PTO as a reward recognizes their professional achievements and supports a healthy work-life balance, which is attractive to job seekers and essential for retaining talent.

- Competitive Advantage: In a competitive job market, businesses that offer unique and attractive benefits like performance-based PTO can stand out. It can be a key differentiator that sets your company apart from others and attracts top talent looking for more than just a paycheck.

- Retention: Earning additional PTO over time creates a sense of loyalty and commitment among employees. They are less likely to leave the company if they have accumulated significant earned time off. This can reduce turnover and the associated costs of recruitment and training.

- Employee Engagement: The prospect of earning extra PTO can enhance employee engagement. When employees have a clear path to earning rewards tied to their performance, they are more likely to stay focused, committed, and invested in the company's success.

- Flexibility and Customization: This approach allows employees to tailor their rewards based on their preferences and needs. Some may take extended vacations, while others may use their earned PTO for shorter breaks or special occasions. The flexibility in using their earned time off can make it even more appealing.

- Motivation and Productivity: Knowing they can earn additional PTO can boost motivation and productivity. Employees are likely to go the extra mile, take on more responsibility, and contribute innovative ideas when they see a direct link between their efforts and rewards.

- Alignment with Company Goals: This approach aligns individual performance with the company's goals and objectives by tying additional PTO to business contributions. It reinforces the idea that everyone's efforts contribute to the company's success, creating a sense of purpose and unity among the workforce.

- Positive Workplace Culture: Rewarding employees with additional PTO for their contributions can help create a positive workplace culture where appreciation and recognition are central values. This culture can foster a sense of belonging and camaraderie, making employees more likely to stay with the organization.

PTO that includes earning additional paid time off based on business contributions and productivity attracts talent and fosters a motivated and committed workforce. It aligns individual and company goals while promoting work-life balance and overall job satisfaction, making it a valuable strategy for talent retention and attraction.

Chapter 3: Sponsorship in important areas:

Supporting employees in areas that are important to them demonstrates an investment in their professional and personal growth. Providing opportunities for training, development programs, or further education can help employees enhance their skills, advance their careers, and feel valued by the organization.

Sponsoring initiatives aligned with employees' interests or causes they care about also fosters a sense of purpose and connection, boosting morale and loyalty.

- Investment in Growth: By sponsoring initiatives related to an employee's professional development, such as training, development programs, or further education, the organization invests in enhancing that individual's skills and expertise. This benefits the employee and strengthens the company's workforce, making it more capable and competitive.

- Career Advancement: Providing opportunities for skill development and career advancement clearly signals that the organization wants its employees to succeed and progress within the company. Employees are more likely to stay with an employer that supports their career aspirations.

- Valuing Employees: When an organization sponsors activities or programs aligned with an employee's interests, it sends a message that it values the individual as a worker and a whole person. This recognition of the employee's passions and personal growth aspirations fosters a sense of appreciation and loyalty.

- Enhanced Skills: Employees who receive sponsorship for skill development can become more valuable assets to the company. They can bring new knowledge and expertise to their roles, potentially leading to innovation, efficiency improvements, and better problem-solving.

- Increased Engagement: Sponsoring initiatives important to employees can increase their engagement at work. When they see that their employer cares about their interests and passions, they are likelier to be enthusiastic and committed to their jobs, leading to higher productivity.

- Alignment with Personal Values: Supporting causes or initiatives that align with an employee's personal values can create a profound sense of purpose. When individuals feel their work is making a positive impact on issues they care deeply about, it can boost morale and motivation.

- Fostering Connection: Sponsorship in areas of personal importance can create a sense of community and connection within the workplace. Employees with common interests or causes can bond over their passions, leading to stronger teamwork and collaboration.

- Attraction and Retention of Talent: Organizations that actively support their employees' growth and personal interests tend to attract and retain top talent. Job seekers often seek employers who align with their values and offer personal and professional development opportunities.

- Adaptation and Innovation: Sponsoring employees' growth in areas important to them can lead to innovative thinking and adaptation. Employees encouraged to explore their interests may develop new ideas and approaches that benefit the organization.

- Overall Wellbeing: Supporting employees in their personal and professional growth contributes to their overall well-being. When employees feel that their needs and aspirations are considered, they are more likely to experience job satisfaction and reduced stress.

Sponsorship in areas important to employees is a strategic investment that pays dividends in employee engagement, skills enhancement, retention, and overall workplace satisfaction. It demonstrates a commitment to employees' holistic growth and well-being, strengthens the employer-employee relationship and creates a more motivated and loyal workforce.

Section 3

Understanding Human Behavior

Ah, yes, understanding human behavior, the elusive art of deciphering the enigmatic minds of our fellow Homo sapiens. It's a field of study that's about as straightforward as navigating a maze blindfolded, only this maze is constantly changing, and the blindfold is made of banana peels.

But fear not, dear reader, for we are about to embark on a delightful journey into the whimsical world of human behavior, a realm where logic takes a long vacation and common sense is often on an extended coffee break.

You see, it's quite a simple task to fathom the intricacies of quantum physics, decode the mysteries of the cosmos, or even master the art of interpretive dance compared to comprehending the quirks and quagmires of the human psyche. After all, humans are the only species that can simultaneously crave social interaction while vehemently desiring solitude, detest change yet constantly seek novelty, and passionately insist on the importance of punctuality while being chronically late for everything.

So, please sit back, relax, and prepare to be thoroughly amused as we embark on this epic quest to grasp the profound mysteries of human behavior. Remember, the road ahead may be fraught with paradoxes, contradictions, and the occasional facepalm-inducing revelation, but hey, what's life without a bit of laughter, right?

Chapter 1: The Importance of Human Behavior in Business

In business leadership, understanding human behavior is crucial for achieving success. Human behavior refers to the actions, attitudes, and emotions individuals or groups display within a social or organizational context. As businesses are fundamentally built on interactions between people, comprehending human behavior becomes a fundamental aspect of effective leadership.

Definition of Human Behavior

Human behavior is a complex and multifaceted subject that draws upon psychology, sociology, anthropology, and other disciplines. It encompasses how individuals act, think, and feel in response to internal and external stimuli. Business leaders must recognize that human behavior is not uniform; it varies based on culture, upbringing, personality, and individual differences.

Therefore, a nuanced understanding of human behavior is necessary for effective leadership.

Role of Human Behavior in Business Leadership

Business leaders who acknowledge the significance of human behavior can utilize this knowledge to enhance decision-making, foster strong relationships, and create a positive organizational culture.

Business leaders who grasp the importance of human behavior can harness this knowledge to make informed decisions, build robust relationships with their teams and stakeholders, and cultivate a positive organizational culture. Furthermore, understanding their limitations empowers leaders to make more self-aware choices, seek assistance or delegate appropriately when necessary, and maintain their well-being, ultimately contributing to their effectiveness and the overall success of their organizations.

Therefore, this dual awareness of human behavior and boundaries is essential for holistic leadership and sustainable business growth.

The role of human behavior in business leadership can be broken down into several key aspects:

- Decision Making: In any organization, leaders must make critical decisions that can impact the business's growth and success. Understanding the behavioral patterns of employees and stakeholders allows leaders to anticipate their reactions to various choices, enabling more informed and well-calibrated decisions.

- Motivation and Productivity: Human behavior is closely tied to motivation and productivity. Leaders who grasp the factors that drive their team members can inspire them to perform at their best. Recognizing individual preferences for work styles, recognition, and rewards can lead to a more engaged and productive workforce.

- Conflict Resolution: Conflicts are inevitable in any workplace. Awareness of a team's different personalities and communication styles can help leaders navigate conflicts effectively and promote harmony among team members.

- Organizational Culture: A company's culture significantly influences how its employees behave and interact. Leaders who understand human behavior can shape a positive and inclusive culture that fosters collaboration, creativity, and employee well-being.

Why Understanding Human Behavior Matters for Business Success

A business is success heavily depends on the people who run it. Individuals build organizations, and employees serve customers. Therefore, understanding human behavior is critical for the following reasons:

- Employee Engagement and Retention: Satisfied and engaged employees are more likely to stay committed to an organization, reducing turnover and the associated costs. Understanding their needs and providing a supportive environment can enhance retention rates and overall employee satisfaction.

- Effective Leadership: A leader who comprehends human behavior can adapt their leadership style to suit different team members. This flexibility leads to more effective communication, collaboration, and employee development.

- Customer Relations: Business leaders must understand customer behavior to effectively meet their needs and preferences. Customer feedback and behavior analysis can inform product development, marketing strategies, and customer service initiatives.

- Team Dynamics: High-performing teams rely on effective team dynamics. Leaders who understand human behavior can build cohesive sections where members complement each other's strengths and work collaboratively towards shared goals.

- Innovation and Adaptability: The business landscape is constantly evolving. Leaders who understand human behavior can foster a culture of innovation and adaptability, encouraging employees to embrace change and think creatively.

- Human behavior is a fundamental aspect of business leadership that should not be overlooked. Leaders who grasp the intricacies of human behavior can make better decisions, motivate their teams effectively, and create a positive work environment that ultimately leads to business success.

Leaders can build stronger relationships and cultivate a thriving organization by understanding and empathizing with their employees and customers.

Chapter 2: The Basics of Human Behavior

The Importance of Self-Awareness for Business Leaders

Self-awareness is critical for business leaders as it enables them to recognize their emotions, strengths, weaknesses, and biases. Through self-awareness, leaders can gain insight into how their behavior and decisions impact others and the organization as a whole. This understanding allows leaders to foster authentic leadership styles, build trust with their teams, and make more mindful and empathetic decisions.

Grasping the basics of human behavior through psychology and understanding individual differences and personality traits are essential for effective business leadership. By considering cognitive, social, and emotional factors, leaders can create a positive work environment, motivate employees, and make informed decisions that lead to the organization's success.

Moreover, cultivating self-awareness allows leaders to enhance their own leadership capabilities and build strong, collaborative teams.

Psychology and Business Leadership

In the context of business leadership, psychology plays a crucial role in understanding and effectively managing human behavior. Psychology is the scientific study of the mind and behavior, delving into the complexities of how individuals perceive, think, feel, and act. As a business leader, applying psychological principles can help decipher employees' and stakeholders' motivations, reactions, and interactions, leading to more informed and empathetic leadership.

The relevance of psychology to business leadership lies in its ability to shed light on the underlying factors that drive human behavior within organizations. By comprehending the psychology behind individual and group dynamics, leaders can optimize their decision-making processes, build stronger teams, and foster a positive work environment that promotes productivity and well-being.

Several key psychological concepts are particularly relevant to business leadership:

- Perception: How individuals interpret and make sense of the world around them significantly influences their behavior in the workplace. Business leaders must know the potential for different perceptions among team members and stakeholders, which can impact communication and decision-making.

- Motivation: Understanding employees' motivation is crucial for enhancing their engagement and productivity. Motivation can be influenced by intrinsic factors (e.g., personal growth, autonomy) and extrinsic factors (e.g., rewards, recognition).

- Learning and Conditioning: People's behavior can be shaped through learning experiences and conditioning. Leaders can utilize this knowledge to implement training programs, reinforce positive behavior, and encourage skill development.

- Social Influence: Human behavior is also strongly influenced by the social context. Social norms, peer pressure, and group dynamics can impact how individuals behave within a team or organization.

- Emotional Intelligence: Emotional intelligence refers to the ability to recognize, understand, and manage one's own emotions and the emotions of others. Leaders with high emotional intelligence can foster better relationships and create a supportive work environment.

The Influence of Cognitive, Social, and Emotional Factors on Behavior

Cognitive, social, and emotional factors all contribute to human behavior in the business setting:

- Cognitive Factors: These encompass mental processes

such as perception, memory, problem-solving, and decision making. A leader's cognitive abilities impact their ability to process information, make sound judgments, and strategize effectively.

- Social Factors: People are inherently social beings, and their interactions with others significantly influence their behavior. Understanding social dynamics within a team or organization can help leaders build cohesive and collaborative teams.

- Emotional Factors: Emotions play a significant role in shaping behavior. Positive emotions can boost creativity and motivation, while negative emotions can hinder performance. Leaders who recognize and address the emotional needs of their employees can create a more supportive and productive work environment.

Individual Differences and Personality

Every individual is unique, and these individual differences play a crucial role in shaping behavior within the workplace. Personal experiences, values, beliefs, and upbringing all contribute to the diverse behaviors displayed by employees and stakeholders. As a result, business leaders must embrace diversity and inclusivity while managing individual differences effectively.

Understanding Personality Traits and Their Impact on Leadership Effectiveness

Personality traits are enduring patterns of thoughts, feelings, and behaviors that distinguish individuals. Different personality traits can influence leadership styles and effectiveness. For instance:

- Extroverted leaders may excel in roles that require strong communication and relationship-building skills.

- Conscientious leaders are often organized, detail-oriented, and dependable, effectively managing complex projects.

- Openness to experience can lead to innovative thinking and a willingness to embrace change, making leaders more adaptable in dynamic business environments.

Understanding the personality traits of oneself and team members can help leaders leverage strengths, identify potential challenges, and adapt their leadership approach accordingly.

The Importance of SelfAwareness for Business Leaders

Self-awareness is critical for business leaders as it enables them to recognize their emotions, strengths, weaknesses, and biases. Through self-awareness, leaders can gain insight into how their behavior and decisions impact others and the organization. This understanding allows leaders to foster authentic leadership styles, build trust with their teams, and make more mindful and empathetic decisions.

Grasping the basics of human behavior through psychology and understanding individual differences and personality traits are essential for effective business leadership. By considering cognitive, social, and emotional factors, leaders can create a positive work environment, motivate employees, and make informed decisions that lead to the organization's success.

Moreover, cultivating self-awareness allows leaders to enhance their leadership capabilities and build strong, collaborative teams.

Chapter 3: Motivation and Engagement

Motivation and engagement are the dynamic duo of the corporate world. It's like trying to catch a unicorn with a butterfly net—elusive, borderline mythical, and often leaving you questioning your life choices. But fear not, my eager beavers of ambition, for we're about to dive headfirst into the bottomless abyss of workplace enthusiasm, a place where enthusiasm goes to play hide-and-seek, and engagement is about as common as a snowstorm in the Sahara.

In this enchanting journey, you'll discover the art of motivating employees, a task as straightforward as herding caffeinated cats in a room full of laser pointers. We'll also explore the fascinating realm of engagement, where the promise of pizza in the break room can sometimes feel like the Holy Grail of workplace perks.

So, strap on your imaginary superhero capes, as we venture into the land of PowerPoint presentations, team-building exercises that induce more eye rolls than enthusiasm, and motivational speeches that could rival a lullaby contest in terms of putting you to sleep. Remember, in the world of motivation and engagement, sarcasm might just be the secret sauce to surviving the madness with your sanity intact.

Theories of Motivation

Motivation is a driving force that compels individuals to act in pursuit of their goals and desires. In the context of business leadership, understanding and applying motivational theories is vital for fostering a highly engaged and productive workforce. Motivated employees are more committed, creative, and satisfied with their work, leading to increased organizational performance and success.

Introduction to Motivation and Its Significance in Business Leadership

Motivation lies at the core of human behavior in the workplace. When motivated employees invest their time and effort into their tasks, leading to improved performance and efficiency. Business leaders who recognize the importance of motivation can harness this energy to drive innovation, improve teamwork, and achieve organizational goals.

Major Motivational Theories

Several prominent theories of motivation provide insights into the factors that drive human behavior in the workplace:

- Maslow's Hierarchy of Needs: Abraham Maslow proposed a hierarchical model of human needs, comprising five levels: physiological, safety, love/belonging, esteem, and self-actualization. According to Maslow, individuals must satisfy lower-level needs before pursuing higher-level ones. Business leaders can apply this theory by ensuring employees' basic needs are met, such as fair compensation, a safe working environment, and opportunities for social connections and professional growth.

- Herzberg's Two-Factor Theory: Frederick Herzberg identified two factors influencing employee satisfaction and dissatisfaction: hygiene factors (e.g., salary, working conditions) and motivators (e.g., recognition, responsibility, personal growth). Leaders should focus on both aspects, striving to eliminate hygiene factors that cause dissatisfaction while emphasizing motivators to enhance employee engagement.

- Expectancy Theory: Proposed by Victor Vroom, the expectancy theory posits that individuals are motivated to act based on their beliefs about the outcomes of their actions. It suggests that employees will be motivated if they believe their efforts produce desirable rewards or outcomes. Leaders can apply this theory by clarifying performance expectations and linking rewards to achievements to boost employee motivation.

- Equity Theory: Developed by J. Stacy Adams, the equity theory suggests that employees compare their inputs (e.g., effort, skills) and outcomes (e.g., pay, recognition) with those of their peers. If they perceive an inequity, it can lead to demotivation and reduced performance. Leaders must ensure fairness in the distribution of rewards and recognition to maintain employee motivation.

Applying Motivation Theories to Enhance Employee Engagement and Productivity

- To enhance employee engagement and productivity, business leaders can apply these motivational theories through various strategies:

- Offer Competitive Compensation: Providing fair and competitive salaries, benefits, and rewards helps satisfy employees' physiological and security needs, reducing financial stress and increasing motivation.

- Recognize and Reward Performance: Acknowledging employees' accomplishments and providing timely recognition reinforces positive behavior and motivates them to excel in their roles.

- Provide Opportunities for Advancement: Creating clear career development paths and opportunities for growth allows employees to pursue their self-actualization needs, leading to higher job satisfaction and motivation.

- Foster a Supportive Work Environment: A positive and supportive work culture, where employees feel valued and heard, can lead to stronger social connections and a sense of belonging, fulfilling their social needs.

Creating a Motivating Work Environment

Several factors contribute to employee motivation and engagement:

- Leadership: Supportive and transformational leadership styles that emphasize empowerment and Success Sponsorship can boost employee motivation and foster a sense of purpose.

- WorkLife Balance: Encouraging work-life balance through flexible work arrangements and wellness initiatives helps prevent burnout and maintains employees' motivation.

- Opportunities for Skill Development: Providing opportunities for learning and skill development allows employees to grow professionally and increases their competence and motivation.

- Collaborative Team Environment: Promoting teamwork and open communication fosters a sense of belonging and shared purpose among team members.

Strategies for Fostering a Positive Work Culture and Supportive Leadership

Business leaders can create a motivating work environment through the following strategies:

- Establish Clear Goals and Expectations: Clearly defining performance expectations and aligning them with organizational objectives helps employees understand their role in contributing to the company's success.

- Encourage Employee Autonomy: Allowing employees autonomy and decision-making authority increases their sense of control and motivation.

- Provide Regular Feedback: Regular feedback and constructive criticism help employees gauge their progress and improve performance, fostering continuous growth and motivation.

- Promote WorkLife Integration: Encouraging work-life integration, where employees can effectively manage work and personal responsibilities, supports their overall well-being and motivation.

The Role of Incentives, Recognition, and Career Development in Motivating Employees

Incentives, recognition, and career development play significant roles in motivating employees:

- Incentives: Well-designed incentive programs, such as performance-based bonuses or commission structures, can motivate employees to strive for excellence and achieve specific targets.

- Recognition: Recognizing employees' efforts and achievements, whether through verbal praise, awards, or public acknowledgment, boosts their morale and reinforces positive behavior.

- Career Development: Providing opportunities for skill enhancement and career growth enables employees to envision a future with the organization, increasing their motivation to perform at their best.

Motivation and engagement are critical components of effective business leadership. By understanding and applying motivational theories, leaders can create a work environment that fosters engagement, productivity, and employee satisfaction.

By emphasizing factors such as recognition, incentives, and career development and promoting a positive work culture, leaders can cultivate a motivated and engaged workforce that contributes to the organization's overall success.

Chapter 4: Communication and Interpersonal Skills

Effective Communication in Leadership

Effective communication is the cornerstone of successful leadership in any business setting. It involves the skillful exchange of information, ideas, and emotions between leaders, team members, and other stakeholders. As a business leader, the ability to communicate effectively is essential for building trust, aligning goals, and fostering a positive work environment.

The Importance of Effective Communication for Business Leaders

Effective communication is crucial for several reasons:

Clear Direction: Communication enables leaders to articulate their vision, goals, and expectations clearly, ensuring that all team members are on the same page.
Alignment and Engagement: When employees understand their roles and how they contribute to the organization's success, they are more engaged and motivated to perform at their best.

Conflict Resolution: Open and honest Communication helps address conflicts and misunderstandings promptly, preventing them from escalating and affecting team dynamics.
Decision Making: Effective Communication facilitates the exchange of information and diverse perspectives, leading to more informed and well-rounded decision-making.

Verbal and Nonverbal Communication Skills

Effective communication encompasses both verbal and nonverbal skills:

Verbal communication involves using words, tone, and language to convey messages. Business leaders should strive for clarity, simplicity, and authenticity in verbal communication.

Nonverbal Communication: Nonverbal cues, such as body language, facial expressions, and gestures, can significantly influence how a message is perceived. Leaders must be mindful of their nonverbal cues to align with verbal communication.

Overcoming Barriers to Communication in the Workplace

- Communication barriers can hinder effective leadership. Some common barriers include:

- Lack of Clarity: Vague or ambiguous messages can lead to confusion and misinterpretation. Leaders should be concise and specific in their communication.

- Poor Listening: Active listening is essential for understanding others' perspectives and concerns. Leaders should practice attentive and empathetic listening.
- Cultural Differences: In diverse workplaces, cultural barriers may impact communication. Leaders should promote inclusivity and sensitivity to different cultural norms.

- Information Overload: Too much information at once can overwhelm recipients. Leaders should prioritize critical information and deliver it in manageable segments.

Overcoming barriers to communication in the workplace is essential for fostering a productive and harmonious work environment. Here are some common barriers and examples of how to overcome them:

- Language and Cultural Barriers:
Example: In a multicultural workplace, employees might speak different languages or have varying cultural norms. To overcome this, offer language training, cultural sensitivity workshops, and encourage open dialogue to bridge gaps.

- Physical Barriers:
Example: If employees work in different locations, use video conferencing, collaboration tools, or regular face-to-face meetings to maintain effective communication and build relationships.

- Technological Barriers:
Example: When technology malfunctions or employees lack digital skills, provide training and support to ensure everyone can use the tools effectively.

- Perceptual Barriers:
Example: People may interpret the same information differently. Clarify messages, encourage feedback, and use visual aids or diagrams to ensure common understanding.

- Emotional Barriers:
Example: A team member might be reluctant to share concerns or feedback due to fear of repercussions. Foster a psychologically safe environment where employees feel comfortable expressing themselves without fear of negative consequences.

- Noise and Distractions:

Example: In a noisy workplace, establish quiet zones, use noise-canceling headphones, or implement a clear signal (e.g., a "do not disturb" sign) when someone needs focused time for communication or work.

- Information Overload:

Example: When overwhelmed with too much information, prioritize messages, communicate concisely, and set clear expectations for response times to avoid burnout.

- Lack of Feedback:

Example: Employees may not provide feedback if they feel it won't be acted upon. Create a culture that values and acts on feedback, and acknowledges and reward employees for their contributions.

- Hierarchical Barriers:

Example: In hierarchical organizations, subordinates may fear retribution for speaking up. Encourage open communication channels, anonymous feedback mechanisms, and leadership accessibility.

- Physical Barriers:

Example: Employees working in different time zones can face scheduling challenges. Implement flexible work hours or establish overlapping core hours for better collaboration.

- Gender or Diversity Bias:

Example: Discrimination can impede open communication. Promote diversity and inclusion, provide diversity training, and address bias through policies and procedures.

- Generational Differences:

Example: Different generations may have distinct communication preferences. Foster cross-generational understanding and adapt communication methods to suit the preferences of various age groups.

- Lack of Trust:
Example: In workplaces with low trust, build trust through transparency, consistency, and demonstrating trustworthiness in actions and decisions.

- Time Constraints:
Example: When everyone is busy, finding time for meaningful communication can be challenging. Schedule regular check-ins and prioritize communication as a part of daily routines.

- Personal Barriers:
Example: Personal issues or stress can affect communication. Encourage employees to seek support, provide resources like counseling, and offer flexibility during difficult times.

Overcoming communication barriers often requires a combination of strategies, including training, creating a supportive culture, and implementing practical solutions to address specific challenges.

Tailoring your approach to your organization's unique needs is essential for effective communication in the workplace.

Emotional Intelligence and Interpersonal Skills

Understanding Emotional Intelligence and Its Impact on Leadership

Emotional intelligence (EI) is the ability to recognize, understand, and manage one's emotions and effectively navigate the emotions of others. EI plays a significant role in effective leadership, influencing how leaders connect with their teams, respond to challenges, and create a positive work environment.

Leaders with high emotional intelligence are better equipped to:
- Empathize with their team members, showing understanding and support
- Communicate with empathy and sensitivity, considering the emotions of others
- Regulate their emotions in high-pressure situations to maintain composure
- Respond to conflicts with emotional maturity and seek constructive resolutions

Developing Empathy, Active Listening, and Conflict Resolution Skills

Developing empathy, active listening, and conflict resolution skills is vital for business leaders:

- Empathy: Understanding and sharing team members' feelings helps leaders build trust and create a supportive work environment. Empathetic leaders are better attuned to their employees' needs and concerns

- Active Listening: Active listening involves giving full attention to the speaker, asking clarifying questions, and providing feedback. Leaders who actively listen can better comprehend their team members' perspectives and address their concerns effectively

- Conflict Resolution: Conflict is inevitable in any workplace. Leaders with strong conflict resolution skills can navigate disagreements constructively, promote collaboration, and maintain team cohesion

Building Strong Relationships and Fostering Collaboration

Interpersonal skills are vital for building strong relationships and fostering collaboration:

- Building Trust: Trust is the foundation of strong relationships. Leaders should demonstrate integrity, reliability, and transparency to earn the trust of their team members

- Collaboration: Encouraging open communication and teamwork fosters a collaborative environment where team members can share ideas and work together effectively

- Appreciation and Recognition: Acknowledging and appreciating the contributions of team members boosts morale and strengthens relationships

Effective communication and interpersonal skills are fundamental for successful business leadership. Leaders who communicate, listen actively, and display emotional intelligence can build strong relationships, foster collaboration, and create a positive work environment.

By overcoming communication barriers and developing empathetic conflict resolution skills, leaders can inspire and motivate their teams to achieve collective success.

Chapter 5: Leading and Managing Teams

Leading and managing teams – it's like trying to organize a group of highly motivated and incredibly self-directed individuals who don't need any guidance whatsoever. Who needs a shepherd when you have a team of thoroughbred unicorns that can magically align themselves with your goals, right?

In this thrilling adventure we call team leadership, you'll discover the fine art of convincing your team that they want to do the work they were hired for, and that yes, attending those "mandatory" meetings is a life-altering experience they shouldn't miss. It's a bit like herding... err, I mean, orchestrating a synchronized swimming routine with dolphins – graceful, effortless, and never involving any splashing or chaos.

But don't worry, we won't delve into the clichés of "team building" or mention trust falls, because we all know that trust is something that can only be built when you're dangling precariously from a tree branch and praying that Bob from accounting has a steady grip.

So, prepare to dive headfirst into the fascinating world of leading and managing teams, where the road to success is paved with sarcasm, humor, and the occasional eye roll – just the way leadership was meant to be!

Team Dynamics and Group Behavior

Teams are essential components of modern organizations, and their effectiveness significantly impacts organizational performance. A team is a group of individuals working together towards a common goal, combining their skills, knowledge, and expertise to achieve shared objectives. Understanding team dynamics and group behavior is critical for business leaders to build cohesive and high-performing teams.

The Nature of Diverse Teams and Their Impact on Organizational Performance

Diverse Teams offer several advantages to organizations:

- Diverse Perspectives: Teams bring together individuals with different backgrounds, experiences, and expertise, leading to a broader range of ideas and solutions

- Collaboration: Effective teamwork fosters collaboration, enabling team members to complement each other's strengths and support each other's weaknesses

- Synergy: When teams work well together, they can achieve more collectively than the sum of individual efforts, creating synergy

- Adaptability: Teams can respond more effectively to complex challenges and dynamic business environments due to their collective problem-solving abilities

A well-functioning team can significantly impact organizational performance, increasing productivity, innovation, and employee satisfaction.

Stages of Team Development and Challenges Faced by Leaders

Teams typically go through several stages of development:

- Forming: In this stage, team members come together, get to know each other, and define their roles and responsibilities. Leaders play a crucial role in clarifying objectives and establishing clear expectations

- Storming: During this stage, conflicts and disagreements may arise as team members adjust to their roles and responsibilities. Leaders must address conflicts constructively and facilitate open communication

- Norming: Team members find common ground, develop group norms, and work more collaboratively. Leaders should encourage mutual respect and cooperation

- Performing: At this stage, the team operates at its highest level of productivity, effectively achieving its goals. Leaders should provide support, feedback, and recognition to maintain performance

- Adjourning: For temporary teams, this stage involves winding down the team after accomplishing its objectives. Leaders should celebrate achievements and acknowledge team members' contributions

Strategies for Building HighPerforming Teams

To build high-performing teams, leaders can adopt the following strategies:

- Define Clear Goals: Communicate the team's objectives, roles, and expectations clearly to ensure alignment and focus

- Foster Open Communication: Encourage transparent and respectful communication to facilitate idea sharing and problem solving

- Promote Psychological Safety: Create an environment where team members feel safe to express their opinions and take calculated risks

- Recognize and Celebrate Achievements: Acknowledge team members' efforts and celebrate successes to boost morale and motivation

- Provide Opportunities for Skill Development: Invest in team members' professional growth to enhance their capabilities and contribution to the team

Leadership Styles and Team Motivation

Leadership styles significantly impact team motivation and performance:

- Authoritative Leadership: Leaders who use an authoritative style provide clear direction and make decisions independently. This approach can be effective in crises but may stifle creativity and autonomy in team members

- Participative Leadership: Participative leaders involve team members in decision-making, encouraging their input and ideas. This style fosters engagement and ownership in the team's goals

- Transformational Leadership: Transformational leaders inspire and motivate their teams through a shared vision and values. They encourage creativity, innovation, and a sense of purpose

- Servant Leadership: Servant leaders prioritize the needs of their team members and aim to support and empower them. This approach builds trust and commitment among team members

Adapting Leadership Approaches to Individual and Team Needs

Effective leaders recognize that different situations and individuals require varying leadership approaches. Adapting leadership styles to individual and team needs can lead to improved motivation and performance:

- Situational Leadership: Leaders assess the competence and commitment of team members and adjust their leadership style accordingly. For example, a team member who is new to a task may require more guidance, while an experienced team member may need more autonomy

- Individualized Support: Leaders should take the time to understand their team members' strengths, aspirations, and concerns. Providing personalized support and recognition fosters a sense of belonging and motivation

- Empowerment: Empowering team members by delegating tasks, providing autonomy, and recognizing their achievements enhances their motivation and commitment to the team's goals

Inspiring and Empowering Teams to Achieve Their Full Potential

Inspiring and empowering teams involves:

- Setting a Compelling Vision: Articulate a clear and inspiring vision that aligns with the team's objectives and resonates with its members

- Providing Resources and Support: Ensure that the team has the necessary resources, training, and support to accomplish its goals effectively

- Encouraging Innovation: Foster a culture of innovation

and creativity where team members are encouraged to think outside the box and take calculated risks

• Celebrating Team Success: Acknowledge and celebrate team achievements to boost morale and foster a sense of accomplishment

Leading and managing teams require a deep understanding of team dynamics, group behavior, and effective communication. By recognizing the stages of team development and the challenges leaders face, business leaders can implement strategies to build high-performing teams.

Adapting leadership styles to individual and team needs, inspiring team members, and empowering them to reach their full potential contribute to team motivation and success.

Through effective team leadership, business leaders can drive organizational performance, innovation, and collaboration, ultimately leading to sustainable growth and success.

Chapter 6: Decision Making and Problem Solving

Oh, the riveting world of the Psychology of Decision Making! Buckle up, because we're about to embark on a journey into the minds of human beings, those flawless ideals of rationality and impeccable judgment. It's a realm where every choice is made with impeccable logic, devoid of biases, emotions, or irrationality.

Who needs Freud when we can all make decisions as effortlessly as calculating the square root of 17 in our heads, right?
Prepare to be amazed as we delve into the intricacies of

decision-making, where every individual always selects the most optimal option, never second-guesses themselves, and never falls victim to the myriad of cognitive biases that don't exist. Yes, folks, welcome to a world where humans are basically walking supercomputers, processing information flawlessly to make choices that shame even the most advanced AI algorithms.

So, if you're ready to explore this utopian land of perfectly rational decision-makers, where choices are made with the precision of a laser-guided missile, you're in for a treat. Because clearly, studying the Psychology of Decision Making is just a formality to confirm what we already know: humans are the epitome of flawless decision-making machines.

The Psychology of Decision Making

Decision-making is a critical aspect of business leadership, involving choosing the best course of action among various alternatives. However, cognitive biases and heuristics often influence human decision-making, leading to suboptimal choices. Understanding the psychology of decision-making can help business leaders make more effective and informed decisions.

Cognitive Biases and Heuristics That Influence Decision Making

Cognitive biases are inherent tendencies in human thinking that can lead to systematic errors in judgment. Some common cognitive biases that affect decision-making include:

*   Confirmation Bias: The tendency to seek and favor information that supports preexisting beliefs, while disregarding contradictory evidence

- Overconfidence Bias: The tendency to overestimate one's abilities and the accuracy of judgments, leading to overconfident decision making

- Anchoring Bias: The tendency to rely heavily on the first piece of information encountered when making decisions, even if it is irrelevant or arbitrary

- Availability Heuristic: The tendency to make judgments based on readily available information in memory, rather than on a full and accurate assessment of all relevant data

Rational Decision Making Models and Their Limitations

Rational decision-making models aim to maximize outcomes by considering all available information and alternatives. However, these models have limitations:
- Time Constraints: In complex business environments, leaders may not have sufficient time to gather and analyze all relevant information before making decisions

- Bounded Rationality: Due to cognitive limitations, individuals may not be able to process all available information, leading to simplified decision making

- Emotional Factors: Emotions can significantly influence decision making, leading to choices that deviate from purely rational considerations

Making Effective Decisions in Complex Business Environments

To make effective decisions in complex business environments, leaders can adopt the following strategies:

- Recognize Cognitive Biases: Being aware of cognitive biases can help leaders avoid their pitfalls and make more objective decisions

- Gather Diverse Perspectives: Encourage input from diverse team members to gain different viewpoints and challenge potential biases

- DataDriven Decision Making: Rely on data and evidence to support decision making, minimizing the impact of subjective biases

- Scenario Analysis: Consider multiple possible outcomes and scenarios to prepare for contingencies and uncertainties

Problem Solving Strategies and Creativity

Approaches to Problem Solving and Decision Making in Business

Problem solving is integral to decision making, as leaders must address challenges and obstacles to achieve desired outcomes. Effective problem solving strategies include:

- Define the Problem: Clearly articulate the problem and its underlying causes to ensure a focused and accurate approach

- Generate Alternatives: Brainstorm and explore various solutions and alternatives to the problem

- Evaluate Alternatives: Assess the strengths and weaknesses of each alternative, considering potential risks and benefits

- Make the Decision: Based on the evaluation, select the most suitable solution and implement it

- Monitor and Adjust: Continuously monitor the results of the decision and be prepared to adjust if necessary

Enhancing Creative Thinking and Innovation in Leadership

Fostering creativity and innovation in leadership can lead to novel solutions and improved decision making:

- Encourage Diverse Perspectives: Embrace diversity in your team, as different perspectives can lead to more innovative ideas

- Create a Supportive Environment: Cultivate a culture where team members feel safe to share their creative ideas and take calculated risks

- Provide Time for Reflection: Allocate time for brainstorming and creative thinking, away from daily operational pressures

- Emphasize Learning and Experimentation: Encourage experimentation and learning from failures, as they are essential parts of the creative process

Encouraging a Culture of Continuous

Improvement

Leaders can promote a culture of continuous improvement by:

- Celebrating Success: Acknowledge and celebrate successful problem-solving efforts and innovation to inspire further improvements

- Providing Resources: Allocate resources for training, research, and development to support ongoing improvement initiatives

- Encouraging Feedback: Welcome feedback from team members, customers, and stakeholders to identify areas for improvement

- Leading by Example: Demonstrate a commitment to continuous improvement by seeking opportunities for growth and development as a leader

Effective decision making and problem solving are vital skills for business leaders. Understanding the psychology of decision-making can help leaders mitigate cognitive biases and make more informed choices. By adopting problem solving strategies and fostering creativity and innovation, leaders can address challenges and seize opportunities in complex business environments.

Encouraging a culture of continuous improvement ensures that the organization stays adaptive, resilient, and continually strives for excellence.

 Chapter 7: Leading Change and

Managing Conflict Change Management and Resistance

Change is an inevitable aspect of organizational life, and successful business leaders must effectively lead change initiatives. However, change often encounters resistance from employees and stakeholders, making change management a complex and critical leadership skill.

Understanding the Dynamics of Change in Organizations

Organizational change can take various forms, including technological advancements, restructuring, process improvements, and strategic shifts. Understanding the dynamics of change involves recognizing that change can be disruptive and create uncertainty among employees. Leaders must clearly communicate the need for change, outline its benefits, and address concerns to gain support.

Common Sources of Resistance to Change and Strategies to Overcome Them

Resistance to change can arise from various sources, including fear of the unknown, loss of control, perceived lack of benefits, and individual or group interests. To overcome resistance, leaders can employ several strategies:

- Communication and Transparency: Keep employees informed throughout the change process, addressing questions and concerns honestly

- Involvement and Empowerment: Involve employees in

the decision-making process when feasible, empowering them to contribute and take ownership of the change

- Training and Support: Provide necessary training and support to help employees adapt to the changes effectively

- Celebrate Quick Wins: Recognize and celebrate early successes to build momentum and confidence in the change initiative

Leading Successful Change Initiatives as a Business Leader

To lead successful change initiatives, business leaders should:

- Develop a Clear Vision: Clearly articulate the purpose and objectives of the change, outlining the expected outcomes

- Create a Change Management Plan: Develop a comprehensive plan that includes communication strategies, training, and support

- Address Concerns and Resistance: Actively listen to employee concerns and address them with empathy and understanding

- Monitor Progress and Adapt: Continuously assess the progress of the change initiative, making adjustments as needed

Conflict Resolution and Negotiation

Identifying and Managing Interpersonal and Intergroup Conflicts

Conflict is inevitable in human interactions, and business leaders must be skilled in identifying and managing conflicts that arise within teams or between groups. Conflict can result from differences in opinions, goals, and task approaches.

To manage conflicts effectively, leaders can:

- Encourage Open Communication: Create an environment where team members can express their concerns and disagreements freely

- Identify Root Causes: Understand the underlying issues contributing to the conflict to address them effectively

- Mediate and Facilitate: Act as a neutral mediator to facilitate constructive discussions and find common ground

Negotiation Techniques for Resolving Conflicts and Reaching WinWin Solutions

Negotiation is a valuable skill for resolving conflicts and reaching mutually beneficial outcomes. Some negotiation techniques include:

- Collaborative Problem Solving: Work together with conflicting parties to identify creative solutions that meet both parties' interests

- Compromise: Find middle ground solutions that involve

concessions from both parties

- Avoidance: When a conflict is not significant or can be resolved by other means, avoiding confrontation may be an appropriate strategy

- WinWin Mindset: Focus on creating outcomes that benefit all parties involved, rather than seeking to "win" at the expense of others

Building Consensus and Maintaining Positive Relationships During Conflicts

- During conflicts, leaders can foster consensus and maintain positive relationships by:

- Emphasizing Common Goals: Remind conflicting parties of shared objectives to encourage cooperation

- Showing Empathy and Understanding: Demonstrate empathy and understanding towards each party's perspective

- Appreciating Diverse Opinions: Acknowledge the value of different viewpoints and encourage respectful dialogue

- Reinforcing Team Cohesion: Strengthen the team's sense of unity and common purpose despite the conflict

Leading change and managing conflict are essential skills for effective business leadership. Leaders must understand the dynamics of change, anticipate resistance, and implement strategies to overcome it. Conflict resolution and negotiation skills enable leaders to address disagreements constructively and foster a positive work environment.

By embracing change as an opportunity for growth and

encouraging open communication and collaboration, leaders can create a resilient and harmonious organizational culture that thrives in the face of challenges.

Chapter 8: Ethical Leadership and Corporate Social Responsibility

Ethical Decision Making in Business

Ethical leadership is a fundamental aspect of effective business management, as it involves making decisions and taking actions that align with moral principles and values. Ethical leaders prioritize financial performance and consider their choices' impact on stakeholders, society, and the environment.

Ethical decision-making is crucial for building trust, credibility, and long-term sustainability in organizations.

The Importance of Ethical Leadership in Building Trust and Credibility

Ethical leadership is vital for building trust and credibility among employees, customers, investors, and other stakeholders. When leaders consistently demonstrate integrity, transparency, and accountability, they inspire confidence in their decisions and actions. Trust is the foundation of strong relationships and effective teamwork, essential for organizational success.

Ethical leaders are role models, and their ethical behavior sets the tone for the organization. Employees are more likely to emulate ethical conduct when they observe ethical leadership from the top.

Trust in leadership fosters employee loyalty, commitment, and engagement, improving job satisfaction and organizational performance.

$\mathfrak{Section}$ 4

Motivational Psychology

Yes, the riveting world of psychological motivational theories! Brace yourselves for a journey into the labyrinthine depths of the human psyche, where we will unravel the mysteries of why people do what they do.

Who wouldn't want to delve into the exciting realm of abstract concepts and mind-boggling theories attempting to explain the most irrational and unpredictable human existence: motivation?

But fear not, for we are about to embark on a thrilling adventure through the annals of psychology, where we'll encounter more theories than you can shake a self-help book at. From Maslow's Hierarchy of Needs, which suggests that we're all just trying to reach the pinnacle of self-actualization, to Herzberg's Two-Factor Theory, which asserts that we're only truly motivated when we don't hate our jobs, we've got it all covered.

So, sit back, relax, and prepare to be utterly fascinated by the mind-bending world of Psychological Motivational Theories. Or not. After all, who needs motivation when sarcasm is the best motivation of all? Furthermore, we've concentrated solely on initiating three highly pragmatic theories.

Classic Drive Theory

In psychology, the intricacies of human motivation have long captivated scholars and thinkers. The classic Drive Theory is among the foundational theories illuminating the landscape of motivation. This chapter delves into the depths of this theory, uncovering its principles, implications, and enduring relevance in understanding the forces that propel human action.

Unearthing the Essence of Drive Theory

Proposed by Clark Hull in the early 20th century, Drive Theory posits that biological needs and internal psychological states drive human behavior. At its core, the theory asserts that deficiencies in basic physiological needs create tension, known as a "drive," which compels individuals to engage in behaviors that reduce or eliminate these deficits and restore equilibrium.

Drive Theory outlines a sequence of events: a physiological need creates a state of arousal, this arousal triggers a drive, and individuals are motivated to act in ways that alleviate the drive and satisfy the need. A classic example is the biological need for food, which generates a hunger drive that prompts individuals to seek and consume nourishment.

Components of Drive Theory

- Drives: Drives arise from physiological imbalances, such as hunger, thirst, or the need for sleep. These internal states propel individuals to seek actions that alleviate discomfort and restore equilibrium.

- Cues: Cues are external stimuli that trigger the initiation of behaviors to satisfy a drive. For instance, the sight or smell of food can act as cues for a hungry individual.

- Response: The response is an individual's behavior to address the drive. In hunger, the response could be seeking, obtaining, and consuming food.

- Rewards: Completing a response leads to rewards, which reduce the drive and bring the individual back to equilibrium. In the case of hunger, the reward is the satisfaction of eating.

Implications and Application

Drive Theory offers valuable insights into various human behaviors, from basic survival instincts to complex decision-making. Its principles have been applied in various fields, including psychology, economics, marketing, and education.

In education, understanding students' basic needs and the drives associated with learning can inform teaching strategies. For instance, addressing students' physiological needs for comfort and safety can create an environment conducive to effective learning.

In marketing, Drive Theory is foundational to the concept of consumer motivation. Advertisers often tap into individuals' needs and drives to create messaging that resonates and compels action, such as using images of delicious food to trigger hunger drives.

Critiques and Limitations

While Drive Theory provides valuable insights, it has been criticized for oversimplifying the complexities of human motivation. Critics argue that it doesn't account for the influence of social and cognitive factors on behavior, such as the role of emotions, culture, and personal values. Drive Theory's strict focus on reducing physiological tensions may not fully explain behaviors beyond basic survival needs, such as engaging in creative pursuits or charitable actions.

Drive Theory remains a fundamental pillar in studying human motivation, offering a lens through which we can understand how biological needs influence behavior. While modern theories have expanded our understanding to encompass the complexities of human motivations, Drive

Theory's legacy is a foundational framework that paved the way for deeper explorations into the multifaceted forces that drive human action.

Self-Determination Theory

Within the intricate tapestry of human motivation, one theory has emerged as a guiding light: Self-Determination Theory (SDT). This chapter delves into the depths of SDT, illuminating its principles, implications, and profound insights it provides into the driving forces behind human behavior.

The Genesis of Self-Determination Theory

Self-Determination Theory, developed by psychologists Edward L. Deci and Richard M. Ryan in the 1980s, offers a comprehensive framework for understanding human motivation and well-being. At its core, SDT emphasizes the role of intrinsic motivation—the inherent desire to engage in activities for personal satisfaction and growth—in shaping behavior and fostering psychological well-being.

Basic Tenets of Self-Determination Theory

Intrinsic and Extrinsic Motivation: SDT categorizes motivation into two distinct types: intrinsic and extrinsic. Intrinsic motivation arises from internal desires, curiosity, and a sense of accomplishment, while extrinsic motivation is driven by external factors such as rewards or social approval.

Basic Psychological Needs: SDT posits that individuals have three fundamental psychological needs: autonomy, competence, and relatedness. Satisfying these needs fosters intrinsic motivation and enhances overall well-being.

Autonomy: Autonomy refers to the sense of volition and choice in one's actions. When individuals feel control over their choices, their motivation becomes more intrinsic. Competence: Competence is the belief in one's ability to effectively navigate and accomplish tasks. Feeling competent in a task boosts intrinsic motivation and encourages engagement.

Relatedness: Relatedness pertains to the sense of connection and belonging with others. Positive social interactions and relationships fulfill the need for relatedness, enhancing motivation and well-being.

Implications and Real-World Applications

Self-Determination Theory's implications span various fields, offering insights influencing education, workplace dynamics, sports, and personal development.

Educators can nurture intrinsic motivation by allowing students to make choices, providing opportunities for competence building, and creating a supportive and inclusive classroom environment.

In the workplace, fostering autonomy by allowing employees to have a say in their tasks, acknowledging their competence, and promoting a sense of belonging can lead to higher job satisfaction and productivity.

Well Being and Flourishing

Self-determination theory isn't just about motivation and enhancing human wellbeing. When individuals' basic psychological needs are met, they experience enhanced vitality, lower stress levels, and greater overall life satisfaction. This theory highlights the importance of fostering environments that encourage intrinsic motivation and support individuals' quest for personal growth and fulfillment.

Critiques and Ongoing Research

While self-determination theory has garnered widespread acclaim, it's not without critiques. Some argue that cultural differences may influence the applicability of the theory's principles across diverse populations. Additionally, striking a balance between intrinsic and extrinsic motivations can sometimes be complex.

Ongoing research explores how SDT interacts with other theories and factors, such as goal setting, emotions, and cognitive processes. This interdisciplinary approach enriches our understanding of motivation and its intricate ties to human behavior.

Self-Determination Theory stands as a shining light in the motivation landscape, illuminating the pathways to human wellbeing and flourishing. By highlighting the significance of intrinsic motivation and the fulfillment of basic psychological needs, SDT provides a profound framework that reshapes how we perceive and cultivate motivation in ourselves and others. As it continues to inspire research and application, Self Determination Theory's legacy persists, reminding us that human motivation is not just a force—it's a fundamental essence that shapes the trajectory of our lives.

Goal Setting Theory

In motivation and accomplishment, a particular theory serves as a strategic guide steering individuals toward success: the Goal Setting Theory. This chapter delves into the fundamental principles, ramifications, and the profound influence of goal setting on human behavior and achievements.

Origins and Foundations of Goal Setting Theory

Developed by psychologists Edwin A. Locke and Gary P. Latham in the 1960s, Goal Setting Theory asserts that specific and challenging goals motivate individuals to achieve higher performance levels. This theory has redefined how we perceive and pursue success by setting clear objectives and delineating a path to accomplishment.

Key Tenets of Goal Setting Theory

Clear Goals: The theory emphasizes setting specific and well-defined goals. Clear objectives give individuals a sense of direction and purpose, fostering motivation.
Challenging Goals: Goals that stretch individuals beyond their comfort zones and require effort are more likely to inspire commitment and determination.
Feedback and Accountability: Regular feedback and monitoring of progress are essential. Individuals are motivated by seeing their advancements and receiving acknowledgment for their efforts.
Goal Commitment: When individuals actively commit to their goals, they become personally invested in their achievement, increasing their intrinsic motivation.

The Power of Goal Setting in Practice

Goal Setting Theory has far-reaching implications across various domains, from personal development to education, sports, and organizational management.
In education, students benefit from setting academic goals. Specific targets, such as achieving a certain grade or completing a project, provide direction and a sense of purpose.

In the workplace, organizations that promote goal setting among employees often witness improved performance and increased job satisfaction. Clearly defined goals align individual efforts with organizational objectives.

Motivation and Cognitive Processes

Goal Setting Theory goes beyond mere external rewards; it taps into intrinsic motivation by fostering a sense of personal accomplishment. As individuals experience progress toward their goals, they derive satisfaction from their efforts, propelling them to persist.

Cognitively, goal setting enhances focus and attention. When individuals have a clear target, their cognitive resources are directed toward relevant tasks, minimizing distractions and optimizing performance.

Critiques and Ongoing Research

While Goal Setting Theory has proved immensely influential, it's not immune to critique. Some argue that overemphasizing challenging goals could lead to stress and burnout. Context and individual differences, such as personality and self-efficacy, can influence the effectiveness of goal-setting strategies.

Ongoing research delves into the intersection of Goal Setting Theory with other motivational theories, examining how factors like self-regulation, feedback, and the complexity of goals impact their achievement.

In human achievement, Goal Setting Theory stands as a steadfast navigator, steering individuals through the complexities of motivation and success. By setting clear, challenging objectives and nurturing the commitment to achieve them, individuals harness the power to transform aspirations into accomplishments.

As this theory inspires research and application, its legacy persists, reminding us that goals aren't just aspirations— tangible roadmaps guiding us toward our greatest achievements.

Section 5

The Psychology and Benefits of Habit Formation

What a joyous occasion! Gather all you diligent, disciplined, and perfectly formed corporate automatons for today. We embark on a thrilling journey into the riveting world of Habit Formation in the workplace. Get ready to unlearn everything you thought you knew about personal responsibility because we're about to delve into the groundbreaking art of spoon-feeding adults and the basics of human behavior.

Yes, ladies and gentlemen, because after years of navigating the treacherous waters of adulthood, paying bills, and maybe even raising kids, you still need someone to tell you how to establish a routine. It's a good thing you've found your way to this guide, where we'll reveal the closely guarded secrets to developing habits so simple that even a trained circus elephant could master them.

But fear not, for our expert instructors, Tim & Andreas, are here to lead you through the complex labyrinth of habit formation. After all, who needs self-motivation when you can have a PowerPoint presentation and a stern talking-to by the water cooler? The ability to create habits, those elusive things that separate us from the animal kingdom, is a skill that can be spoon-fed to you in a one-hour seminar.

So, prepare to have your minds blown, dear readers, as we teach you the life-altering skill of Habit Formation, a concept so advanced and nuanced that it requires a guide to understand. After all, who wants to rely on their willpower when they can follow a step-by-step guide and call it a day?

***

The psychology of habit formation encompasses a range of positive attributes that can profoundly impact our lives. First and foremost, it provides us with a powerful tool for personal growth and self-improvement.

By understanding the mechanisms behind habit formation, we can deliberately cultivate positive routines and behaviors. Habits help automate actions, making it easier to maintain consistency in our efforts, whether adopting a healthier lifestyle, becoming more productive, or enhancing our skills.

Moreover, habits can provide stability and routine in our daily lives, reducing decision fatigue and stress. They promote discipline, resilience, and perseverance, as they often require gradual effort and persistence to establish. Ultimately, the psychology of habit formation empowers us to control our actions, positively and constructively shaping our destinies.
In the ever-evolving landscape of modern businesses, an organization's success largely hinges upon its employees' collective habits. Good and bad habits play a significant role in shaping productivity, efficiency, and overall well-being within the workplace. Thus, instilling the knowledge and tools to form positive habits and discern when negative ones need to be amended is paramount.

Fostering a culture of self-awareness and continuous improvement, businesses can empower their workforce to optimize performance, cultivate personal growth, and ultimately achieve tremendous success in their endeavors.

This section delves into the critical reasons why teaching employees how to cultivate good habits and identify and transform detrimental ones is essential, leading to a more resilient, engaged, and thriving workforce.

The time it takes to form a new habit in a process-driven business can vary depending on various factors. While there is no fixed duration, research suggests that it generally takes an average of 66 days for a habit to become automatic and ingrained in an individual's behavior.

Coaching employees on habit formation for routine tasks is essential for several reasons:

- Efficiency and productivity: Developing habits allows employees to perform routine tasks efficiently and consistently. When employees have established habits, they can complete their work more quickly, reducing the time and effort required for repetitive tasks. This leads to increased productivity and a more efficient workflow within the organization.

- Consistency and quality: Habits help establish a consistent approach to performing tasks. When employees consistently follow a set of habits, they are more likely to deliver consistent, high-quality results. This is particularly important for jobs that require attention to detail or adherence to specific standards or processes.

- Time and resource management: Habit formation helps employees manage their time and resources effectively. When employees have established habits for routine tasks, they can prioritize their work, allocate resources efficiently, and avoid unnecessary delays or wastage. This can result in better time management, improved resource allocation, and overall cost savings for the organization.

- Reduced cognitive load: By turning routine tasks into habits, employees can reduce the cognitive load associated with decision-making and task execution. Habits operate on autopilot, freeing up mental energy and allowing employees to focus on more complex or critical aspects of their work. This can contribute to better decision-making, problem-solving, and creativity in other areas of their job.

- Adaptability and agility: When employees have well-established habits for routine tasks, they become more adaptable and agile in handling changes or disruptions. As the business environment evolves, employees with ingrained habits can quickly adapt to new circumstances, processes, or technologies without significant disruptions to their performance. This enhances the organization's ability to respond to changing market conditions or customer demands.

- Employee empowerment and autonomy: Coaching employees on habit formation empowers them to take ownership of their work and develop a sense of independence. When employees have the skills and knowledge to establish effective habits, they feel more confident in their abilities and have greater control over their work. This can lead to higher job satisfaction, increased motivation, and improved employee engagement.

Coaching employees on habit formation for routine tasks can positively impact efficiency, productivity, quality, and employee satisfaction. By helping employees develop effective habits, organizations can optimize their performance and achieve better results in the long run.

How Long Does It Take To Form a New Habit?

The time it takes to form a new habit in a process-driven business can vary depending on various factors. While there is no fixed duration, research suggests that it generally takes an average of 66 days for a habit to become automatic and ingrained in an individual's behavior.

However, this timeline can differ based on several factors, including:

- Complexity of the habit: The complexity of the habit being formed can impact the time it takes to establish it. Simple habits may be formed more quickly, while complex ones require more time and effort.

- Consistency and frequency: Regular and consistent practice is essential for habit formation. The more frequently an action is repeated, the more likely it becomes a habit. In a process-driven business, if employees consistently engage in the desired behavior, it can expedite the habit formation process.

- Individual differences: Everyone is different, and habit formation can vary based on personal characteristics, motivation, prior experiences, and learning styles. Some employees may adopt new habits more quickly than others.

- Organizational culture and support: The corporate culture and support for habit formation can significantly influence the speed at which habits are established. If there is a supportive environment, clear expectations, and adequate resources for training and reinforcement, it can facilitate habit development.

It's important to note that while habits can be formed in a few months, sustaining them requires ongoing reinforcement, monitoring, and support. Organizations can implement strategies such as providing training, setting goals, offering incentives, and providing feedback to help employees develop and maintain desired habits in a process-driven business.

Chapter 1: Efficiency, Productivity, Consistency & Quality

Creating good employee habits is crucial to reducing process variation within a business, leading to significant cost savings and improved customer satisfaction. By their nature, habits promote consistency and reliability in behavior, which directly impacts the efficiency and effectiveness of business processes. Employees who develop positive habits are more likely to follow standardized procedures, make fewer errors, and deliver consistent results. Here's how forming good habits contributes to reducing process variation and its subsequent benefits:

Standardization and Reproducibility

Good habits encourage employees to follow standardized procedures and best practices consistently. By adhering to established guidelines, processes become more predictable and reproducible. This uniformity minimizes variations in output, ensuring that customers receive consistent, high-quality products or services, which boosts customer satisfaction.

Standardization and reproducibility are essential aspects of good habits in business. They involve creating and following consistent processes and procedures to ensure uniformity and reliability in the delivery of products or services.

Here's a detailed explanation of why standardization and reproducibility are vital components of good habits that benefit both the business and its customers:

- Consistency in Quality: Employees who follow standardized procedures and best practices produce consistent output. This consistency ensures that each product or service meets the same high-quality standards, eliminating the risk of variations that could lead to subpar results. Customers value consistency in quality, as it builds trust and confidence in the business's offerings.

- Predictable Results: Standardized processes enable businesses to predict outcomes with a higher degree of certainty. The results are more reliable and predictable since employees are trained to follow specific steps and guidelines. This predictability is crucial in meeting customer expectations and avoiding unexpected errors or defects.

- Efficiency and Productivity: Following standardized procedures streamlines workflows and reduces the time and effort required for each task. When employees know the most efficient way to carry out their responsibilities, they can complete their work faster and more accurately. Increased efficiency leads to higher productivity, allowing the business to handle more orders or serve more customers within the same time frame.

- Training and Onboarding: Standardized processes make it easier to train new employees and facilitate smooth onboarding. With clear and documented procedures to follow, new hires can quickly learn how to perform their roles effectively. This reduces the learning curve and ensures that the quality of work remains consistent, even with personnel changes.

- Continuous Improvement: Standardized processes provide a solid foundation for continuous improvement initiatives. When processes are clearly defined and documented, it becomes easier to identify areas for enhancement and optimization. Businesses can analyze data, gather feedback, and make informed adjustments to improve efficiency and meet changing customer needs.

- Scalability and Growth: Standardization is essential for businesses aiming to scale and grow. As the demand for products or services increases, standardized processes allow the business to maintain consistency and reliability in its offerings. This scalability is crucial for expanding into new markets and attracting more customers.

- Regulatory Compliance: In industries with strict regulations and standards, standardized processes help ensure compliance with legal requirements. By adhering to established guidelines, businesses can demonstrate their commitment to meeting industry standards and providing safe and reliable products or services.

- Brand Reputation: A reputation for delivering consistent and high-quality products or services positively impacts the brand's image. Customers are more likely to trust and recommend a business with a reputation for reliability. This positive brand perception can increase customer loyalty and give a company a competitive advantage in the market.

Standardization and reproducibility are crucial components of good habits in business because they contribute to consistent quality, predictability, efficiency, and reduced errors.

They facilitate training and onboarding, support continuous improvement efforts, and enhance scalability and compliance. Ultimately, these habits lead to improved customer satisfaction and a strong brand reputation, positioning the business for long-term success and growth.

Simplify: Minimize Mistakes and Corrections

With good habits, employees are more attentive and less prone to errors. By consistently performing tasks in a structured manner, they are less likely to overlook critical steps or make avoidable mistakes. This decrease in errors leads to less rework, saving time, effort, and resources.

Good habits are crucial in reducing errors and rework for employees in various ways. When employees develop and adhere to positive habits, they become more attentive, disciplined, and proactive in their approach to tasks and responsibilities. This heightened sense of focus and consistency significantly reduces errors and the need for rework. Here's how good habits contribute to this positive outcome:

- Attention to Detail: Good habits often involve being detail-oriented and thorough in work processes. By consistently paying attention to the finer points of tasks, employees are less likely to overlook critical steps or make careless mistakes that could lead to errors.

- Consistency in Procedures: Positive habits encourage employees to consistently follow standardized procedures and best practices. This consistency ensures that employees carry out tasks uniformly, minimizing the likelihood of errors resulting from deviation from established protocols.

- Effective Time Management: Developing good habits in time management allows employees to allocate sufficient time for each task. When employees have ample time to complete their work, they can do so without rushing, reducing the risk of errors caused by haste or lack of focus.

- Continuous Improvement: Good habits foster a culture of continuous improvement, where employees actively seek feedback and identify areas for enhancement. By proactively addressing weaknesses and learning from mistakes, employees can minimize the occurrence of errors in the future

.

- Clear Communication: Positive habits often involve effective communication skills, which reduce the chances of misunderstandings and misinterpretations. By ensuring clarity in instructions and expectations, employees can avoid errors caused by miscommunication.

- Reduced Procrastination: Good habits discourage procrastination and promote timely task completion. When employees start and finish tasks promptly, they have more time to review their work and catch any errors before they escalate.

- Adherence to Quality Standards: Developing good habits includes a commitment to maintaining quality standards at work. When employees prioritize quality over speed, they are more likely to take the necessary precautions to avoid errors and ensure work meets expectations.

- Increased Accountability: Embracing good habits fosters a sense of responsibility and accountability. When employees take ownership of their work and outcomes, they are more motivated to double-check their work, reducing the chances of errors.
- Training and Skill Development: Good habits involve a dedication to continuous learning and skill development. As employees improve their proficiency, they become more competent in their roles, leading to fewer errors due to a lack of knowledge or expertise.

- Positive Work Environment: A work environment that encourages good habits and supports employee growth fosters a sense of satisfaction and engagement. Employees who feel valued and supported are more likely to be attentive and committed to producing error-free work.

Good habits significantly reduce errors and rework for employees by promoting attention to detail, consistency in procedures, effective time management, continuous improvement, clear communication, reduced procrastination, adherence to quality standards, increased accountability, training, and a positive work environment.

As employees develop and embrace positive habits, the overall quality of work improves, leading to increased efficiency, productivity, and customer satisfaction.

- Streamlined Workflows: Good habits streamline workflows by ensuring that tasks are completed logically, reducing the potential for bottlenecks and delays. As a result, processes move more smoothly and efficiently, leading to faster turnaround times and improved customer response times.

- Employees who develop and practice positive habits prioritize efficiency, organization, and structured approaches to work. These habits create a smooth flow of tasks, minimizing interruptions and ensuring that work progresses seamlessly from one stage to another. Here's how good habits contribute to streamlined workflows:

- Task Prioritization: Good habits encourage employees to prioritize tasks based on their importance and urgency. By identifying high-priority activities and addressing them first, employees can focus on critical tasks, reducing the risk of bottlenecks caused by delays in essential work.

- Structured Workflows: Positive habits often involve adhering to established workflows and processes. When employees follow structured procedures, work moves logically from one step to the next, minimizing confusion and inefficiency.

- Clear Communication: Good habits include effective communication skills, which facilitate the exchange of information and instructions between team members. Clear communication ensures everyone knows their roles and responsibilities, preventing misunderstandings that can lead to delays.

- Time Management: Developing good habits in time management helps employees allocate sufficient time for each task. Adequate time allocation prevents rushing through work, reducing the risk of errors and the need for rework, which can cause delays.

- Proactive Problem Solving: Positive habits encourage employees to proactively address challenges and roadblocks. When employees are empowered to tackle issues as they arise, potential bottlenecks can be resolved swiftly, preventing them from impeding the workflow.

- Standardization: Good habits often involve following standardized procedures and best practices. Standardization ensures that work is carried out consistently, regardless of who performs the task, reducing variations that could cause delays.

- Continuous Improvement: Developing good habits includes a commitment to continuous improvement.

By analyzing workflows and identifying areas for enhancement, employees can refine processes to make them more efficient and less prone to bottlenecks.

- Collaboration and Teamwork: Positive habits foster a collaborative culture where team members support each other and work together to overcome challenges. By leveraging collective strengths and expertise, teams can navigate workflow hurdles more effectively.

- Workload Distribution: Good habits involve effectively distributing workloads among team members based on their skills and capacity. Balancing workloads ensures that no one is overwhelmed, reducing the risk of bottlenecks due to an uneven distribution of tasks.

- Task Handoffs: When tasks involve multiple stages or team members, good habits emphasize clear handoffs and communication between individuals. Smooth task handoffs prevent delays and confusion when transferring work from one person to another.

Good habits streamline workflows by ensuring that tasks are completed logically, focusing on prioritization, structured approaches, clear communication, and proactive problem-solving. By adhering to established procedures and fostering a culture of continuous improvement and collaboration, employees can navigate workflows efficiently, reducing the potential for bottlenecks and delays.

As a result, the organization benefits from increased productivity, smoother operations, and improved overall performance.

Consistent Customer Experience

A key benefit of reducing process variation through good habits is creating a consistent customer experience. Customers value reliability and predictability in their interactions with a business. When employees consistently follow established processes, customers can trust that their expectations will be met, increasing satisfaction and loyalty.

Improved Employee Morale

Forming good habits empowers employees to take pride in their work and contribute to the organization's success. As they see the positive impact of their habits on process efficiency and customer satisfaction, their morale improves. High employee morale translates to increased engagement, lower turnover, and a more committed workforce.

Continuous Improvement

Good habits foster a culture of continuous improvement within the organization. As employees consistently engage in processes, they are more likely to identify areas for enhancement and innovation. This culture of continuous improvement allows the business to proactively address challenges, anticipate customer needs, and stay ahead of competitors.

Data-Driven Decision Making

Standardized processes resulting from good habits facilitate data collection and analysis. With consistent data, businesses can make informed, data-driven decisions to optimize operations, identify trends, and proactively address potential issues.

Data-driven decision-making leads to more efficient processes and better allocation of resources.

Creating good habits among employees is a powerful tool for reducing process variation in a business. Consistent adherence to established procedures enhances efficiency, reduces errors, and fosters a culture of continuous improvement. This leads to cost savings and streamlined operations and improved customer satisfaction through a consistent and reliable customer experience.

As businesses focus on developing positive habits within their workforce, they position themselves for long-term success, growth, and a competitive edge in the market.

Chapter 2: Time and Resource Allocation

Good habits play a significant role in optimizing time and resources in business, positively impacting the organization's culture. Employees who develop and embrace productive habits become more efficient, focused, and responsible with their time and resource allocation.

This optimization has a cascading effect on various aspects of the company's culture, fostering an environment of productivity, collaboration, and continuous improvement.

Here's how good habits contribute to these outcomes:

- Time Management and Prioritization: Good habits, such as setting clear goals, creating to-do lists, and adhering to structured routines, enable employees to manage their time effectively. By prioritizing tasks and allocating time efficiently, employees can focus on high-impact activities, leading to increased productivity and better use of time.

- Reduced Procrastination and Distractions: Productive habits instil discipline and self-control, reducing the tendency for employees to procrastinate or succumb to distractions. This enhanced focus leads to faster task completion, reducing time wasted on nonessential activities.

- Streamlined Workflows: Good habits encourage employees to consistently follow standardized procedures and best practices. This consistency streamlines workflows, minimizing unnecessary steps and delays. Streamlined processes lead to quicker turnaround times and better resource utilization.

- Improved Decision-Making: Positive habits often involve seeking feedback, reflecting on past experiences, and making data-driven decisions. When employees develop these habits, they become more adept at making informed choices and taking calculated risks, leading to better resource allocation and more effective problem-solving.

- Resource Optimization: Productive habits extend beyond time management to include resource optimization. Employees who develop the habit of being mindful of resource usage tend to minimize waste and utilize materials, finances, and manpower more efficiently.

- Culture of Accountability: Embracing good habits fosters a culture of accountability, where employees take ownership of their actions and outcomes. In such a culture, employees are more likely to take responsibility for using time and resources effectively, leading to a more responsible and proactive workforce.
- Continuous Improvement: Good habits promote a growth mindset, where employees actively seek ways to improve their skills, processes, and efficiency. This

culture of continuous improvement drives innovation and optimization at all levels of the organization.

- Collaboration and Teamwork: When employees optimize their time and resources, they become more reliable and supportive team members. By working efficiently and meeting deadlines, they contribute to a positive team dynamic, enhancing collaboration and fostering a sense of camaraderie.

- Employee Well-being and Work-Life Balance: Developing good habits in time management and resource optimization can reduce stress levels and improve work-life balance for employees. A culture that values productivity and efficiency while also considering employee well-being creates a more supportive and sustainable work environment.

- Alignment with Company Goals: Good habits encourage employees to align their actions with the company's overall goals and objectives. When time and resources are used strategically, the entire organization moves cohesively toward achieving its mission.

Good habits have a profound impact on optimizing time and resources in business. As employees develop productive habits, they become more focused, disciplined, and efficient in their work. The collective influence of these habits shapes the organization's culture, fostering a sense of accountability, collaboration, and continuous improvement.

Through cultivating positive habits, businesses can create a thriving and productive work environment where employees work together towards shared goals and achieve the greatest impact on overall success.

# Chapter 3: Reducing Cognitive Load

Reducing cognitive load is a groundbreaking and revolutionary concept! Who would have thought that making things simpler and easier to understand could be beneficial? It's not like our brains are already bombarded with constant information and stimuli, right?

So, let's dive into this groundbreaking topic of reducing cognitive load because, clearly, it's something we've all been ignoring up until now.

***

In the fast-paced modern workplace, the ability to make informed and swift decisions is a crucial factor for both individual and collective success. The cognitive load that employees experience can significantly impact their decision-making abilities, influencing not only the quality of their choices but also their overall productivity and the collaborative culture within the organization.

This chapter delves into the cognitive load, its implications on decision-making, and strategies to effectively reduce it, ultimately leading to improved decisions, heightened productivity, and a more harmonious collaborative atmosphere.

Understanding Cognitive Load and Decision-Making

Cognitive load refers to the mental effort required to process information and perform tasks. It is divided into three types: intrinsic, extraneous, and germane. Intrinsic cognitive load pertains to a task's inherent complexity, while extraneous cognitive load relates to unnecessary factors that complicate tasks.

Germane cognitive load, on the other hand, is the productive cognitive effort that aids in learning and problem-solving.

When employees are overwhelmed by cognitive load, their decision-making capacity can be severely hampered. Complex tasks and a barrage of information can lead to decision fatigue, where individuals become mentally exhausted and are more prone to making hasty and suboptimal choices. This can lead to decreased productivity, as valuable time and resources are expended on rectifying poor decisions.

Benefits of Reduced Cognitive Load on Decision-Making

Reducing cognitive load can have profound positive effects on the decision-making process, thus contributing to heightened productivity and a more collaborative work environment:

- Clarity of Thought: Employees who are not weighed down by excessive information or complex tasks can think more clearly and critically. This clarity enables them to evaluate options, anticipate consequences, and make decisions that align with their goals and the organization's objectives.

- Efficient Processing: Organizations can optimize their workflows by minimizing extraneous cognitive load. When employees can focus on essential information without distractions, they can process information more efficiently, leading to quicker and more accurate decision-making.

- Enhanced Creativity: Reducing cognitive load allows employees to tap into their creative reserves. When minds are unburdened by excessive mental strain, individuals are more likely to devise innovative solutions to challenges, contributing to a culture of continuous improvement and problem-solving.

- Collaborative Culture: Reducing cognitive load fosters a more collaborative atmosphere. Not overwhelmed employees are better equipped to engage in meaningful discussions, actively listen to others, and contribute constructively to team projects. This leads to better communication and cooperation among team members.

Strategies for Reducing Cognitive Load

Organizations can implement various strategies to reduce cognitive load and reap the associated benefits:

- Streamlined Information: Provide employees with the necessary information while filtering out irrelevant details. This prevents information overload and ensures that decision-makers clearly understand the situation at hand.

- Training and Skill Development: Equip employees with the skills needed to efficiently process information and manage complex tasks. Enhanced skills lead to increased confidence in decision-making and reduced cognitive strain.

- Decision Support Tools: Implement tools and technologies that provide relevant data and insights. Automation can take over routine tasks, freeing up employees' cognitive resources for more critical thinking.

- Breaks and Mindfulness: Encourage regular breaks and mindfulness practices to alleviate mental fatigue. Short breaks allow employees to recharge, reducing the likelihood of decision fatigue and mistakes.

- Effective Communication: Promote clear and concise communication throughout the organization. Clarity in communication reduces the mental effort required to decipher messages and instructions.

Reducing cognitive load is a powerful strategy that organizations can employ to enhance decision-making, productivity, and collaborative culture in the workplace. By acknowledging the various forms of cognitive load and adopting effective strategies to mitigate them, organizations can create an environment where employees can make better and faster decisions, improving individual and collective performance. This, in turn, contributes to the growth and success of the organization in today's dynamic and competitive business landscape.

Chapter 4: Agility and Adaptability

In an era of rapid technological advancements, shifting market trends, and dynamic business landscapes, the ability to adapt swiftly and effectively is a cornerstone of success for both individuals and organizations.

Developing and nurturing good habits can play a pivotal role in enabling employees and organizations to be more agile in responding to constant market and business needs changes. This chapter delves into the significance of cultivating good habits, their impact on agility, and practical ways to foster a culture of adaptability within the workforce and the organization.

The Power of Good Habits in Navigating Change

Habits are automatic behaviors that are deeply ingrained in our daily routines. When applied strategically, they can be powerful tools for building resilience and adaptability. Good habits that promote productivity, flexibility, and continuous improvement can significantly contribute to an organization's ability to thrive amidst change.

Here's how they facilitate agility:

- Consistency in Learning: Habitual learning is crucial for staying updated with industry trends and market shifts. Employees who establish a habit of continuous learning are better equipped to acquire new skills and knowledge, which are essential for adapting to evolving business needs.

- Efficient Time Management: Habits such as effective time management and prioritization ensure that employees allocate their time and efforts to tasks that align with changing priorities. This prevents wasted time on low-priority tasks and allows quick redirection toward more pressing matters.

- Iterative Improvement: Habits of iterative improvement foster a culture of experimentation and adaptation. Employees and organizations regularly assessing and refining their processes, products, and strategies can swiftly pivot when necessary.

- CrossFunctional Collaboration: Habitual collaboration and open communication enhance an organization's ability to respond to change. When teams are accustomed to working together and sharing insights, they can seamlessly adjust their approaches in response to shifting market dynamics.

Fostering Good Habit Adoption for Agility

Goal-Oriented Mindset: Encourage employees to set clear, achievable goals. Goal-setting habits align individual and team efforts with strategic objectives, enabling focused adaptation to changing market needs.

- Embrace Feedback: Develop a habit of seeking and giving feedback. Constructive feedback aids in identifying areas that require adjustment and drives continuous improvement.

- Agile Methodologies: Implement agile methodologies, such as scrum or kanban, to cultivate incremental progress and flexibility habits. These methodologies promote adaptive planning and teamwork, enabling organizations to respond quickly to changing requirements.

- CrossTraining: Encourage cross-training among employees to develop a diverse skill set. This habit ensures that teams can readily shift responsibilities as needed, enhancing organizational flexibility.

- Reflection and Learning: Instill a habit of regular reflection and learning from both successes and failures. This habit promotes a growth mindset and fuels the adaptability to navigate uncertainties.

- Technology Utilization: Develop habits of leveraging technology for streamlined processes and data-driven decision-making. Technology-enabled processes can be modified swiftly to address emerging challenges.

- Encourage RiskTaking: Cultivate a habit of calculated risk-taking. Employees who feel empowered to take measured risks are more likely to propose innovative solutions and embrace change.

The ever-evolving business landscape demands a proactive and agile approach to adaptation. Employees and organizations can navigate change with confidence and resilience by cultivating good habits that prioritize continuous learning, effective communication, iterative improvement, and flexibility.

These habits equip individuals to respond swiftly to market fluctuations and foster a culture of adaptability permeating the entire organization. In a world characterized by constant change, the cultivation of good habits serves as a compass guiding employees and organizations towards success in the face of uncertainty.

Chapter 5: Empowerment and Autonomy

In today's dynamic workplace, empowering employees to take ownership of their roles and decisions fosters innovation, productivity, and a positive work culture. One powerful approach to achieving this empowerment is through coaching employees on habit formation. This chapter explores the transformative impact of habit formation coaching on empowering employees, granting them greater autonomy, and nurturing their personal and professional growth.

The Dynamics of Habit Formation and Empowerment

Habits are powerful routines that shape behavior and influence outcomes. When employees learn to intentionally cultivate positive habits, they unlock the potential to take control of their actions and responses, leading to enhanced autonomy.

Habit formation coaching equips employees with the tools to understand, develop, and sustain beneficial habits, creating a ripple effect of empowerment:

- Self-Awareness: Habit formation coaching encourages employees to reflect on their current habits, both constructive and counterproductive. This self-awareness empowers them to identify areas for improvement and growth.

- Goal Alignment: Employees can set meaningful goals through coaching and align their habits with these objectives. This alignment fosters a sense of purpose and direction, motivating them to take ownership of their actions.

- Personal Responsibility: Habit formation coaching emphasizes accountability and responsibility. Employees recognize that their habits influence their success, leading to a heightened sense of ownership over their work and decisions.

- Adaptability: Coached employees develop the ability to adapt their habits in response to evolving circumstances. This adaptability enables them to confidently navigate change, making autonomous decisions when facing new challenges.
- Confidence: As employees witness their habits yielding positive results, their self-confidence grows. They feel empowered to tackle complex tasks and challenges, further contributing to their sense of autonomy.

Fostering Autonomy through Habit Formation Coaching

Tailored Guidance: Habit formation coaching begins with personalized guidance. Coaches work closely with employees to understand their goals, strengths, and areas for improvement, providing tailored strategies for habit development.

Goal Setting: Coaches assist employees in setting achievable goals that align with both personal and organizational aspirations. Goal Setting promotes a sense of autonomy, as employees are actively involved in shaping their professional path.

- Actionable Steps: Coaching sessions break down the process of habit formation into actionable steps. Employees learn how to start small, build momentum, and progressively integrate new habits into their routines.

- Positive Reinforcement: Coaches offer positive reinforcement as employees progress in cultivating desired habits. This recognition fuels motivation and reinforces the value of autonomous decision-making.

- Overcoming Obstacles: Habit formation coaching equips employees with strategies to overcome obstacles and setbacks. They learn to problem-solve independently, further enhancing their autonomy.
- Continuous Growth: Coaches encourage employees to view habit formation as a continuous growth journey. This perspective instills a mindset of lifelong learning and adaptation, reinforcing their autonomy.

Cultivating Organizational Culture through Habit Empowerment

As habit formation coaching empowers individual employees, it also contributes to developing a thriving organizational culture.

- When employees are empowered and autonomous, they naturally become more engaged, innovative, and collaborative:

- Collaborative Environment: Empowered employees are more likely to collaborate effectively as they take ownership of their contributions and seek opportunities to share insights and ideas.
- Innovation: Autonomy fosters a conducive environment for innovation. Empowered employees are more inclined to propose novel solutions and experiment with new approaches.

- Resilience: Empowered employees navigate challenges with resilience. Their autonomy equips them to respond to setbacks proactively, adapting their habits and strategies as needed.

- Leadership Development: Habit formation coaching cultivates leadership skills. Empowered employees often take on leadership roles within their teams, inspiring and guiding their colleagues.

- Positive Work Culture: The empowerment and autonomy fostered through habit formation coaching contribute to a positive work culture characterized by trust, transparency, and mutual support.

Habit formation coaching is a transformative approach to employee empowerment that reverberates throughout the organization. Coaching nurtures employees' autonomy, self-efficacy, and sense of responsibility by guiding employees to cultivate positive habits.

As empowered employees take charge of their actions and decisions, they contribute to a dynamic work culture marked by innovation, collaboration, and adaptability. Ultimately, habit formation coaching propels individuals toward growth and success and fuels the collective achievement of organizational goals in an ever-evolving business landscape.

Chapter 6: Habit Loops

A key concept in understanding and optimizing these habits is the habit loop, a psychological framework that consists of three components: cue, routine, and reward. This chapter will delve into the art of creating a workplace plan centered around habit loops. We will explore how to identify existing habits, modify them, and establish new ones to enhance productivity, foster a positive work environment, and achieve both individual and organizational goals.

Understanding Habit Loops

What are Habit Loops?

- Habit loops are repetitive patterns of behavior that are driven by a cue, followed by a routine or action, and concluded by a reward. Understanding this concept is crucial for improving workplace habits. Cues can be internal (emotions, thoughts) or external (alarms, emails), routines are the actions or behaviors triggered by cues, and rewards are the positive outcomes or feelings that reinforce the habit.

The Science Behind Habit Loops

- To create an effective workplace plan on habit loops, it's essential to appreciate the neurological aspects. Habits form in the basal ganglia, a part of the brain responsible for automatic behaviors. When a behavior becomes a habit, it transfers from the more energy-intensive prefrontal cortex to the basal ganglia, making it automatic and less mentally taxing.

Identifying Existing Habits

Self-Reflection and Observation

- Begin by encouraging employees and yourself to reflect on their daily routines and behaviors. What are their go-to reactions to common workplace cues? Are these behaviors contributing positively or negatively to their work performance and well-being? Documenting these habits is the first step in creating a workplace plan.

Collecting Data

- Data-driven insights can be invaluable in identifying existing habits. Use surveys, time-tracking apps, and feedback mechanisms to gather information on how employees spend their time, handle stress, and react to various triggers. Analyzing this data will reveal prevalent habit loops.

Modifying and Optimizing Habits

- Once you've identified existing habits, evaluate their impact. Are there any habits that hinder productivity, teamwork, or employee well-being? These are prime candidates for modification.

Rewiring the Routine

- To modify habits, focus on altering the routine while preserving the cue and reward. For example, if procrastination is a prevalent habit in your workplace (cue: a challenging task, routine: delay, reward: temporary relief), encourage employees to replace procrastination with a more productive routine, such as breaking tasks into smaller, manageable chunks.

Implementing Positive Habits

- Simultaneously, work on establishing new, positive habits that align with your organizational goals. Provide clear cues, design routines that facilitate the desired behavior, and ensure meaningful rewards. For instance, to foster a culture of continuous learning, encourage employees to set aside time each week for skill development (cue: a specific time, routine: learning activity, reward: sense of accomplishment and growth).

Tracking Progress and Adaptation

Monitoring and Feedback

- Regularly assess the progress of habit modifications and new habit formation. Use performance metrics, feedback, and one-on-one meetings to gauge the effectiveness of the workplace plan. Encourage employees to share their experiences and challenges.

Adaptation and Flexibility

Be prepared to adapt the workplace plan as needed. Employee needs and the business environment can change, so the plan should remain flexible. If certain habits don't yield the desired results or new challenges emerge, adjust the cues, routines, or rewards accordingly.

Sustaining and Scaling Habits

Building a Habit-Positive Culture

- To sustain positive habits in the workplace, cultivate a culture that values and reinforces them. Recognize and celebrate successes, share success stories, and encourage peer accountability. Over time, habits become ingrained in the workplace culture.

Scaling Habits Across the Organization

- Once you've successfully implemented habit loops within your team or department, consider scaling these habits across the entire organization. Share best practices, offer training, and establish a framework that promotes habit formation at all levels.

Creating a workplace plan centered around habit loops is a strategic approach to improving productivity, employee satisfaction, and overall organizational success. By understanding, identifying, modifying, and optimizing habits, you can foster a culture of continuous improvement and adaptability, ultimately achieving your workplace goals.

Embrace the science behind habit loops, and your organization will thrive in the ever-evolving corporate landscape.

Section 6

Data-Driven Decision Making

Data-driven decision-making is the magical elixir of modern business! It's like a crystal ball that tells you exactly what to do, as long as you can decipher its cryptic messages and perform a sacred dance while chanting "Correlation does not imply causation" in a dark room lit only by flickering Excel spreadsheets.

Yes, forget about those old-fashioned gut feelings and intuition – who needs 'em? Instead, let's entrust our fate to rows and columns of numbers that were probably generated by a computer without any idea what it's doing. After all, nothing says "I'm a serious decision-maker," like blindly following the gospel of data analytics, right?

Grab your oversized glasses, put on your best pocket protector, and dive headfirst into the thrilling world of data-driven decision-making! It's like a rollercoaster ride with more pie charts and fewer safety harnesses. Who needs common sense when you can have scatter plots and histograms to guide your every move?

So, buckle up decision-makers and prepare to ride the data-driven roller coaster into a future where spreadsheets, graphs, and the occasional magic eight-ball determine everything. Who needs to think when you can just follow the numbers?

***

In today's data-driven world, the power of information has revolutionized decision-making processes across industries and sectors. Harnessing data to inform choices offers a distinct advantage by increasing the statistical probability of achieving successful outcomes. This section delves into the key reasons why data-driven decisions are more likely to yield favorable results, highlighting the objectivity, insights, and risk mitigation capabilities that data brings to the decision-making table.

Using data to make decisions increases the statistical probability of a successful outcome for several reasons:

- Objective Information: Data provides objective and factual information not influenced by biases, emotions, or personal opinions. Decisions based on data are less likely to be swayed by subjective factors, increasing the likelihood of a successful outcome.

- Pattern Recognition: Data analysis allows for identifying patterns, trends, and correlations that may not be apparent through intuition alone. By recognizing these patterns, decision-makers can make more informed choices and anticipate potential outcomes.

- Risk Mitigation: Data can help assess and quantify risks associated with various options or strategies. By understanding the potential risks and their probabilities, decision-makers can take steps to mitigate them or choose alternatives with lower associated risks.

- Evidence-Based Decisions: Data Driven decisions are often grounded in empirical evidence. This means decisions are more likely to be supported by real-world observations, increasing the likelihood that they will align with the actual conditions and circumstances.

- Data-driven Insights: Data analysis tools like statistical models and machine learning algorithms can generate insights that humans might overlook. These insights can provide a competitive advantage and lead to more successful outcomes.

- Continuous Improvement: By collecting and analyzing data, organizations can track the performance of their decisions over time. This feedback loop allows continuous improvement as decisions are refined based on past results and new data.

- Efficiency: Data can help streamline decision-making processes by providing information quickly and efficiently. This can lead to faster and more effective decisions, especially in fast-paced or complex environments.

- Resource Allocation: Data can inform resource allocation decisions. By analyzing resource utilization and performance data, organizations can allocate their resources more effectively, optimizing their chances of success.

- Adaptability: Data-driven decision-making allows for adaptability in rapidly changing situations. Decision-makers can quickly respond to emerging trends or unexpected events using real-time data and analytics.

- Quantitative Assessment: Data provides a basis for quantitative assessment, allowing decision-makers to assign numerical values to various factors. This enables more precise comparisons between different options and their potential outcomes.

- Transparency and Accountability: Data-Driven decisions are often more transparent, as the rationale behind them is grounded in data that can be shared and scrutinized. This transparency fosters accountability and trust among stakeholders.

- Reduced Cognitive Biases: Human decision-makers are prone to cognitive biases like confirmation or anchoring biases. Data can help counteract these biases by providing an objective foundation for decision-making.

Using data to make decisions enhances decision quality by providing a factual, evidence-based foundation that helps identify patterns, quantify risks, and optimize resource allocation. It reduces the influence of biases, fosters transparency, and allows for continuous improvement, all contributing to an increased statistical probability of achieving successful outcomes.

However, it's important to note that data should be collected, analyzed, and interpreted accurately and responsibly to realize these benefits fully.

Chapter 1: The Power of DataDriven Decision Making

In the dynamic landscape of today's world, companies and higher education institutions face ever-increasing complexities and challenges. Organizations must embrace data-driven decision-making to navigate these complexities successfully and achieve sustainable growth and improvement.

This chapter delves into the critical importance of being data-driven, shedding light on how harnessing the power of data can drive excellence and innovation in these sectors.
Having a structured customer database is paramount for companies in today's digital age.

A well-organized database allows businesses to store and access vital customer information efficiently, such as contact details, purchase history, preferences, and interaction history. This accessibility empowers companies to provide personalized and targeted marketing campaigns, offer tailored products or services, and enhance overall customer experiences.

Moreover, a structured database aids in data analysis, enabling companies to make data-driven decisions, identify trends, and forecast customer behavior. Additionally, it enhances data security and compliance by ensuring that sensitive customer information is properly managed and protected. In a nutshell, a structured customer database is not just a convenience but a strategic necessity for companies aiming to thrive in a competitive market and build enduring customer relationships.

The Pervasiveness of Data

Data is all around us. Every interaction, transaction, and process generates valuable information. This data takes various forms, such as customer feedback, enrollment statistics, financial records, and performance metrics. Ignoring this wealth of data means missing out on improvement, innovation, and optimization opportunities.

Realizing Efficiency and Cost Savings

Data Driven decision-making enables organizations to identify inefficiencies and streamline processes. By analyzing data on resource allocation, for example, universities can allocate budgets more effectively, while CX Companies can optimize their service delivery processes. This saves costs and enhances the overall quality of service or education.

Optimizing the Experience Journey

Data-driven decision-making allows organizations to gain insights into these stakeholders' preferences, behaviors, and pain points. By leveraging this information, they can tailor their services, courses, and offerings to meet individual needs, ultimately enhancing the overall experience.

Data-driven decision-making is a critical approach that empowers organizations to delve deeper into the intricacies of their stakeholders' preferences, behaviors, and pain points. This methodology involves systematically collecting, analyzing, and interpreting data to draw meaningful insights. By harnessing this wealth of information, organizations can customize their services, courses, and offerings to cater to each stakeholder's specific needs and desires. This personalization improves customer satisfaction and strengthens brand loyalty and trust.

Understanding the unique characteristics and demands of stakeholders is paramount. Data-driven decision-making enables organizations to pinpoint the exact pain points that might be hindering stakeholder satisfaction. For instance, a company can analyze customer feedback data to identify recurring issues or concerns and then take targeted actions to address them.

This not only resolves immediate problems but also showcases a commitment to continuous improvement, which is highly valued by stakeholders.

Data-driven insights allow organizations to anticipate future trends and adapt proactively. By tracking behavioral patterns and preferences over time, businesses can make strategic decisions that keep them ahead of the curve. For example, an e-learning platform can analyze user data to identify emerging learning trends or preferences, allowing them to develop and offer courses that are in high demand.

In essence, data-driven decision-making is a transformative approach that empowers organizations to stay agile and responsive in a rapidly evolving landscape. It fosters a culture of customer-centricity, enabling companies to meet and exceed stakeholder expectations. By continuously refining their offerings based on data-driven insights, organizations can create a seamless and personalized experience for their stakeholders, resulting in enhanced satisfaction, loyalty, and long-term success.

Predictive Analytics for Strategic Planning

Future planning is essential. Data-driven decision-making enables predictive analytics, which empowers organizations to foresee trends and challenges. For instance, a university can use enrollment data and socioeconomic trends to anticipate student demand for specific programs, enabling it to allocate resources accordingly. Organizations can predict customer trends, allowing them to adapt their offerings proactively.

Focus Feature: CX Companies & Higher Education Institutions

Predictive analytics can be a powerful tool for both Customer Experience (CX) companies and higher education institutions to enhance their strategic planning processes. These organizations can make informed decisions and anticipate future trends by leveraging historical data, statistical algorithms, and machine-learning techniques.

Here's how CX companies and higher education institutions can use predictive analytics for strategic planning:

CX Companies:

- Customer Behavior Analysis: CX companies can use predictive analytics to analyze past customer behavior data. By identifying patterns and trends, they can predict future customer behaviors, such as purchase preferences, interaction channels, and the likelihood of churn. This information can inform product development, marketing strategies, and customer engagement initiatives.

- Demand Forecasting: Predictive analytics can help CX companies forecast demand for their products or services accurately. By analyzing historical sales data and external factors like economic indicators or seasonality, they can optimize inventory management and staffing levels, ensuring they meet customer demands efficiently.

- Customer Segmentation: Predictive analytics can segment customers based on their characteristics, behaviors, and preferences. This segmentation allows CX companies to tailor marketing campaigns and customer experiences more effectively. By understanding the specific needs of different customer segments, they can enhance customer satisfaction and loyalty.

- Personalized Customer Experiences: With predictive analytics, CX companies can create personalized customer experiences. By predicting what products or services a customer is likely to be interested in, they can recommend relevant offerings, leading to higher conversion rates and customer satisfaction.

- Churn Prediction and Retention Strategies: Predictive models can forecast which customers are at risk of churning. CX companies can then implement proactive retention strategies, such as targeted offers or bold customer support, to reduce churn rates and maintain a loyal customer base.

Higher Education Institutions:

- Enrollment and Admissions: Educational institutions can use predictive analytics to forecast enrollment numbers accurately. By analyzing historical enrollment data, demographic trends, and application behaviors, they can adjust marketing efforts, class sizes, and resources to meet future enrollment needs.

- Student Success Prediction: Predictive analytics can identify students who may be at risk of academic struggles or dropping out. By considering factors like attendance, course performance, and demographic information, higher education institutions can implement early intervention programs and support systems to improve student retention and success rates.

- Resource Allocation: higher education institutions can optimize resource allocation by predicting future demands for classrooms, faculty, and support services. This ensures that they can allocate budgets more efficiently and offer a diverse range of courses and programs that meet student needs.

- Curriculum Development: Predictive analytics can help higher education institutions determine which courses and programs are likely to be in high demand. By analyzing student preferences and career trends, institutions can tailor their curriculum offerings to align with market demands and student interests.

- Fundraising and Alumni Engagement: Educational institutions can use predictive analytics to identify potential donors and engage alumni effectively. By analyzing alumni giving history and demographics, higher education institutions can target fundraising campaigns and engagement initiatives, increasing donor contributions.

Predictive analytics empowers both CX companies and higher education institutions to make data-driven decisions and develop more effective strategic plans. By leveraging historical data and advanced analytical techniques, organizations can enhance customer experiences, improve enrollment and retention rates, allocate resources efficiently, and stay ahead of the competition. It's a valuable tool for achieving long-term success and sustainability in these sectors.

Continuous Improvement and Innovation

Continuous improvement serves as a vital force within customer experience-oriented organizations. Employing data-driven decision-making establishes an ongoing feedback mechanism, empowering these organizations to meticulously oversee their performance. Through the scrutiny of data pertaining to student outcomes or customer satisfaction, these entities can pinpoint opportunities for enhancement and introduce innovations to remain competitive and pertinent.

Demonstrating Accountability

In today's environment, accountability is not just a buzzword—it's a necessity. Customer experience-oriented organizations are accountable to various stakeholders, from customers and students to investors and accrediting bodies.

Data Driven decision-making offers a transparent and evidence-based way to demonstrate accountability. It allows organizations to track and report on key performance indicators, providing stakeholders with confidence in their operations.

Chapter 2: Navigating Uncertainty

"Navigating Uncertainty" Because clearly, there's nothing more exhilarating than attempting to steer a ship through a storm without a compass, a map, or even a clue where you're going. But hey, who needs stability, predictability, or a sense of direction when you can have uncertainty, confusion, and a perpetual state of existential dread, right?

In this thrilling adventure, we'll explore the fine art of pretending to know what the heck you're doing while secretly praying that your decisions won't lead to the inevitable downfall of your organization. Because why not make every day at work feel like a high-stakes game of poker?

Forget about the quaint notion of strategic planning, long-term goals, or, heaven forbid, a clear vision for the future. Instead, embrace the chaos, relish in the constant barrage of curveballs, and get ready to pivot, adapt, and pivot some more until you've completely lost track of what your organization actually stands for.

But don't worry, we'll provide you with all the tips and tricks you'll need to excel in the art of ambiguity. You'll learn how to master the art of vague communication, dodge accountability like a pro, and turn every setback into a learning opportunity (or at least a decent excuse).

So, buckle up, fellow adventurers of uncertainty, as we embark on this wild journey through the treacherous waters of organizational chaos. Who needs stability and sanity anyway?

***

The business and educational landscapes are constantly evolving, often in unpredictable ways. Data Driven decision-making equips organizations with the tools to navigate uncertainty. By regularly collecting and analyzing data, they can make agile, informed decisions, mitigating risks and seizing opportunities as they arise.

Uncertainty is a constant in today's business and operational environment, and data-driven decision-making provides organizations with the tools to respond proactively and make informed choices even in uncertain situations. Here's how it helps:

• Fact Based Decision Making:
Uncertainty often leads to anxiety and fear of the unknown. Data-Driven decision-making relies on empirical evidence and facts rather than gut feelings or speculation.

By analyzing historical data and current trends, organizations can make decisions based on real information, reducing the risk of making hasty or misguided choices during uncertain times.

- Risk Mitigation:

Data analysis allows organizations to identify potential risks and vulnerabilities more accurately. They can anticipate possible scenarios and take proactive measures to mitigate those risks.

Risk assessments based on data can help organizations allocate resources more effectively and create contingency plans to handle unexpected events.

- Agility and Adaptability:

Data Driven organizations are more agile and adaptable. They can quickly adjust strategies and tactics as new information becomes available.

During times of uncertainty, such as market fluctuations or unexpected disruptions like the COVID-19 pandemic, data-driven organizations can pivot their operations, marketing, and supply chain management based on real-time data.

- Resource Allocation:

Efficient allocation of resources is critical during uncertain times. Data Driven decision-making helps organizations identify which projects or initiatives are most likely to yield positive returns.

By analyzing data, organizations can prioritize investments, allocate budgets strategically, and ensure they focus on areas that align with their goals and offer the greatest potential for success.

- Scenario Planning:

Data-Driven organizations engage in scenario planning. They create multiple scenarios based on different assumptions and analyze the potential outcomes and impacts of each scenario.

This approach helps organizations prepare for a range of possibilities and develop strategies that are robust and flexible enough to handle various situations.

• Customer and Stakeholder Insights:
During uncertain times, understanding customer behavior and stakeholder expectations is crucial. Data-Driven decision-making enables organizations to gather and analyze customer feedback, preferences, and sentiment.

With this information, organizations can tailor their products, services, and communication strategies to meet changing customer needs and maintain stakeholder trust.

• Continuous Monitoring and Feedback:
Data Driven decision-making is an ongoing process that involves continuous monitoring and feedback. Organizations regularly collect data, assess performance, and adjust their strategies accordingly.

This iterative approach allows organizations to stay attuned to changing conditions and make data-driven decisions as the situation evolves.

• Improved Communication and Transparency:
Data Driven decisions are often more transparent and easier to communicate to stakeholders. Leaders can provide an evidence-based rationale for their choices, which instills confidence in employees, investors, and customers.
Transparency fosters trust and helps organizations maintain strong relationships with their stakeholders during uncertain times.

In customer experience-oriented organizations, being data-driven is not a choice but a necessity for success in today's competitive and dynamic environment. Data is the key to efficiency, cost savings, enhanced customer or student experiences, strategic planning, continuous improvement, accountability, and adaptability.

Organizations that embrace data-driven decision-making will not only survive but thrive, delivering excellence and innovation that set them apart from the competition. The journey toward data-driven excellence begins with a commitment to data collection, analysis, and integration into every aspect of organizational decision-making. By doing so, organizations can chart a course to a brighter and more prosperous future.

Chapter 3: Guide to Ethical Data Collection for Organizations

Data collection is an essential component of modern organizations, enabling them to make informed decisions, improve internal processes, and enhance customer experiences. However, collecting data comes with significant ethical responsibilities. Mishandling data can lead to privacy breaches, erode customer trust, and even result in legal consequences.

To help organizations collect data ethically and responsibly, here is a comprehensive guide:

Establish Ethical Data Collection Principles

- Develop Data Ethics Policies
- Define Your Organization's Ethical Data Principles:

- Create a set of clear, written guidelines that outline your organization's commitment to ethical data collection and usage.
- Appoint Data Ethics Officers: Designate individuals or a team responsible for overseeing data ethics within your organization.
- Understand Legal Requirements
- Comply with Data Protection Regulations: Ensure that you are adhering to relevant data protection laws, such as the General Data Protection Regulation (GDPR), the California Consumer Privacy Act (CCPA), and other applicable regional laws.
- Consent and Transparency: Clearly communicate data collection purposes to individuals and obtain their informed consent where necessary.
- Minimize Data Collection
- Collect Only What Is Necessary: Limit data collection to the minimum required to achieve your organization's objectives.
- Anonymize and Pseudonymize Data: Whenever possible, de-identify data to protect individual identities.

Ethical Data Collection Practices

- Data Collection Methods
- Transparency: Inform individuals about data collection methods, sources, and intentions.
- Data Minimization: Gather data directly from individuals when possible, rather than obtaining it from third-party sources.
- Data Storage and Security
- Data Encryption: Encrypt sensitive data both in transit and at rest to protect it from unauthorized access.
- Access Control: Implement strict access controls to ensure that only authorized personnel can access and manipulate collected data.

- Data Retention
- Define Data Retention Policies: Establish clear timelines for data retention and disposal, adhering to legal requirements.
- Periodic Data Audits: Regularly review stored data to identify and delete obsolete or unnecessary information.

Maintain Ethical Data Usage

- Purpose Limitation
- Use Data for Intended Purposes: Ensure that collected data is used solely for the purposes for which it was collected.
- Consent Management: Implement robust systems for managing and tracking user consent and preferences.
- Data Sharing
- Data Sharing Agreements: When sharing data with third parties, establish clear agreements that outline usage restrictions and data protection measures.
- Data Masking: Before sharing data, consider using techniques like data masking or tokenization to protect individual identities.
- Data Transparency
- Data Privacy Notices: Publish clear and concise data privacy notices that explain data collection, usage, and individual rights.
- Data Access Requests: Establish procedures for individuals to request access to their own data and correct any inaccuracies.

Continuous Improvement and Accountability

- Training and Awareness
- Employee Training: Educate your staff about data ethics, privacy, and security regularly.

- Ethics Awareness Campaigns: Promote data ethics awareness among all stakeholders, including customers and partners.
- Data Breach Response
- Incident Response Plan: Develop a robust plan for responding to data breaches promptly and effectively.
- Notification Protocol: Establish a procedure for notifying affected individuals and regulatory authorities in the event of a data breach.
- Compliance Audits
- Regular Audits: Conduct regular internal audits to ensure compliance with data protection laws and internal policies.
- External Audits: Consider engaging third-party auditors to assess your organization's data protection practices objectively.

Why This All Matters

Ethical data collection plays a pivotal role in building trust not only with customers but also with employees. Here's how it contributes to trust-building:

Building Trust with Customers:

- Transparency: Ethical data collection practices involve being transparent about why data is being collected, how it will be used, and who will have access to it. When customers fully understand the data collection process, they are more likely to trust the organization.

- Respect for Privacy: Ethical data collection respects individuals' privacy rights, such as obtaining informed consent and safeguarding their personal information. Customers appreciate knowing that their data is handled with care and won't be misused.

- Data Security: Ethical data collection involves robust security measures to protect customer data from breaches and unauthorized access. Customers trust organizations that prioritize their data security.

- Data Accuracy: Ethical data practices focus on collecting accurate and relevant data. When customers see that their information is used effectively and without errors, they are more likely to trust the organization's decision-making processes.

- Accountability: Organizations that adhere to ethical data collection principles take responsibility for any data-related issues or breaches. This accountability demonstrates a commitment to rectifying problems and mitigating harm, which builds trust.

- Data Use Consistency: Ethical organizations use customer data only for the purposes for which it was collected. Customers trust that their information won't be exploited for unrelated activities.

- Data Access and Control: Ethical data collection allows customers to have more control over their data. Providing options for customers to access, update, or delete their data fosters a sense of empowerment and trust.

Building Trust with Employees

- Ethical Culture: Ethical data practices reflect an organization's commitment to ethical behavior in all aspects of its operations. This culture extends to how employees are treated and how their data is handled.

- Employee Data Privacy: Just as customers appreciate

data privacy, employees also expect their personal and sensitive information to be handled ethically. Respecting employees' data privacy rights can lead to higher job satisfaction and loyalty.

- Fairness: Ethical data collection ensures that data about employees is used fairly and without discrimination. When employees feel that their data is treated fairly, it contributes to a positive work environment and trust in management.

- Data Security: Employees trust that their data is secure when their organization follows ethical data security practices. This trust is vital, especially in industries where employee data is sensitive, such as healthcare and finance.

- Communication: Ethical data practices often involve clear and open communication within the organization. Employees are more likely to trust leadership when they are kept informed about data policies and procedures.

- Compliance and Accountability: Ethical data practices demonstrate an organization's commitment to complying with laws and regulations. Employees trust that the organization will protect their rights and hold itself accountable for any data-related issues.

- Professional Development: Ethical data use can also benefit employees in terms of professional development. When organizations analyze data ethically, they can make informed decisions that enhance employee experiences, career growth, and job satisfaction.

Ethical data collection is a cornerstone of trust-building, not only with customers but also with employees. Organizations that prioritize ethics in data handling create an environment of transparency, fairness, and accountability, which in turn fosters trust among both customers and employees. This trust is invaluable for long-term success and positive relationships with all stakeholders.

By following the principles and practices outlined in this guide, organizations can collect and use data in a responsible and ethical manner, benefiting both their internal operations and their customers. Always stay vigilant, adapt to evolving data privacy regulations, and prioritize the protection of individuals' rights and privacy.

Chapter 4: Comprehensive Guide to Data Analysis for Organizational Improvement

What a thrilling odyssey awaits you in this "Comprehensive Guide to Data Analysis for Organizational Improvement"! Brace yourselves, for you are about to embark on a riveting adventure into the world of data analysis—a realm so bright that it makes watching paint dry seem like a rollercoaster ride at Disneyland.

In this guide, we will delve deep into the riveting world of numbers, charts, and spreadsheets. Yes, you heard that right! We'll help you unlock the mystical powers of data analysis, transforming your organization into a dazzling beacon of efficiency and excellence. Who needs action-packed novels or binge-worthy TV shows when you can immerse yourself in the thrilling universe of data?

Prepare to be amazed as we unravel the mysteries of statistical significance, regression analysis, and the oh-so-fascinating world of data visualization. Your social life will undoubtedly take a backseat as you become the life of the data party, impressing your friends and family with your newfound expertise.

But wait, there's more! We'll throw in some mind-numbing jargon, mind-boggling equations, and enough pie charts to make you crave a real pie (preferably with extra whipped cream). By the time you finish this guide, you'll be so immersed in data that you'll start seeing spreadsheets in your sleep.
So, ladies and gentlemen, fasten your seatbelts and get ready for a data-driven ride of a lifetime. Who needs adventure sports when you can have the time of your life with numbers and data analysis? Trust us; this guide will make you wish every day was a Monday morning data-crunching session. Enjoy!

***

Data analysis is a crucial process for organizations seeking to enhance their internal operations and deliver better results to their customers. It empowers decision-makers with valuable insights, enabling them to make informed choices, optimize processes, and provide more personalized services. This comprehensive guide will walk you through the steps and best practices to effectively utilize data analysis to improve both internal operations and customer satisfaction.

Understanding the Importance of Data Analysis
Why Data Analysis Matters

Data analysis is the process of examining, cleaning, transforming, and interpreting data to discover valuable insights. It is crucial because it enables organizations to:

- Identify trends and patterns
- Make informed decisions
- Enhance operational efficiency
- Improve customer satisfaction
- Stay competitive in a data-driven world
- Benefits of Data Analysis
- Cost reduction through process optimization
- Increased revenue through better customer targeting
- Improved product and service quality
- Enhanced customer experiences
- Better risk management and fraud detection

Preparing Your Data

- Data Collection

Collect data from various sources, such as internal databases, customer feedback, surveys, and external sources like social media or market research. Ensure data is accurate, relevant, and collected ethically.

- Data Cleaning and Validation

Cleanse data by removing duplicates, handling missing values, and correcting errors. Validate data for accuracy and consistency to ensure reliable analysis

- Data Storage

Store data securely, adhering to data privacy regulations. Consider using cloud-based or on-premises databases and implement data backups and access controls.

Selecting the Right Data Analysis Tools

- Tools for Data Exploration

Use data exploration tools like Microsoft Excel, Google Sheets, or Python libraries (e.g., Pandas) to perform initial data analysis and gain insights.

- Statistical Analysis Software

Employ software like R, SPSS, or Python with statistical packages (e.g., SciPy) for in-depth statistical analysis

- Data Visualization Tools

Utilize visualization tools like Tableau, Power BI, or Matplotlib for creating insightful charts, graphs, and dashboards to present findings effectively

Choosing the Right Metrics

- Key Performance Indicators (KPIs)

Define KPIs that align with your organizational goals, such as revenue growth, customer satisfaction, or operational efficiency.

- Customer-Centric Metrics

Track metrics like Net Promoter Score (NPS), Customer Lifetime Value (CLV), and Customer Churn to understand and improve customer relationships

- Internal Efficiency Metrics

Monitor internal metrics such as employee productivity, resource allocation, and process efficiency to streamline operations.

Exploratory Data Analysis (EDA)

- Descriptive Statistics

Use summary statistics (mean, median, standard deviation) to understand data distributions and central tendencies
- Data Visualization

Create visualizations like histograms, scatter plots, and box plots to explore data visually (A separate section will delve deeper into Data Visualization).

- Hypothesis Testing

Apply statistical tests to verify hypotheses and make data-driven decisions

Advanced-Data Analysis Techniques

- Predictive Analytics

Use historical data to forecast future trends and outcomes, enabling proactive decision-making

- Machine Learning

Implement machine learning models for predictive analytics, classification, and recommendation systems

- Time Series Analysis

Analyze time-based data to identify seasonality and trends

Interpreting Results

• Drawing Meaningful Insights
Translate data findings into actionable insights that align with your organization's goals

• Identifying Patterns and Trends
Look for recurring patterns and emerging trends that may impact your business

• Making Data-Driven Decisions
Ensure that decisions are based on data-driven evidence, not intuition alone

Implementing Changes

• Internal Process Optimization
Apply insights to improve internal operations, streamline processes, and increase efficiency

• Customer-Centric Improvements
Enhance products and services based on customer feedback and preferences

• Setting SMART Goals
Establish specific, measurable, achievable, relevant, and time-bound goals for implementing changes

Monitoring and Iteration

• Continuous Data Analysis
Continuously monitor KPIs and metrics to assess the impact of changes and make necessary adjustments

- Feedback Loops
Gather feedback from employees and customers to inform ongoing improvements

- Adaptation to Change
Be agile and adapt strategies as the business environment evolves

Training and Skill Development

- Building Data Literacy
Promote data literacy across the organization, ensuring that employees understand and value data

- Data Analysis Training Programs
Invest in training programs for data analysts and professionals to enhance their skills

- Hiring Data Analysts
Recruit data analysts or data science experts to support your data analysis efforts

Case Studies

Explore real-world examples of organizations that have successfully used data analysis to improve operations and customer experiences

As projects are implemented within your organization, use them as case studies to enhance credentials and facilitate educational opportunities.

By following this comprehensive guide, organizations can harness the power of data analysis to drive internal improvements and deliver better results to their customers.

Remember that data analysis is an ongoing process, and continuous learning and adaptation are essential for long-term success.

Chapter 5: Guide to Data Integration for Improved Organizational Results

Data integration is a critical component of modern organizations striving for efficiency, informed decision-making, and enhanced customer satisfaction. When executed effectively, data integration can help streamline operations, provide actionable insights, and deliver better experiences for both internal stakeholders and customers.
This guide will outline key steps and best practices to help organizations integrate data successfully into their daily operational framework.

Understanding Data Integration

• What is Data Integration?
Data integration is the process of combining data from various sources, formats, and locations into a unified and accessible format. It involves transforming, cleaning, and storing data in a way that makes it useful for analysis, reporting, and decision-making.

Why is Data Integration Important?

• Improved Decision-Making: Integrated data provides a holistic view of the organization, enabling informed decisions

• Operational Efficiency: Streamlined data processes reduce manual effort and errors

- Enhanced Customer Experiences: Integrated data enables personalized services and faster issue resolution

Preparing for Data Integration

- Define Objectives

Clearly the define the goals and objectives of your data integration project. Understand what you aim to achieve and how integrated data will benefit your organization and customers

- Assess Current Data Ecosystem

Audit existing data sources, systems, and processes. Identify data silos and bottlenecks that hinder integration efforts.

- Secure Necessary Resources

Allocate budget, staff, and technology resources required for data integration. Ensure executive support for the project. Choosing Data Integration Tools and Technologies

- Data Integration Platforms

Select a data integration platform that suits your organization's needs. Options include cloud-based on-premises or hybrid solutions.

- ETL (Extract, Transform, Load) Tools

Choose ETL tools that facilitate data extraction, transformation, and loading processes efficiently.

- API Integration

Leverage APIs to connect applications and data sources, enabling real-time data exchange

Data Integration Best Practices

• Data Quality and Cleansing
Ensure data quality by cleaning, deduplicating, and validating data during integration.

• Data Governance
Implement data governance policies to manage data access, ownership, and compliance.

• Data Mapping and Transformation
Map data fields and apply appropriate transformations to ensure data compatibility.

• Data Security and Compliance
Prioritize data security and comply with relevant regulations to protect sensitive information

• Monitoring and Maintenance
Establish monitoring systems to track data integration processes and resolve issues promptly

Implementing Data Integration

• Data Mapping and Schema Design
Create data maps and define data schemas to structure integrated data

• Data Extraction and Transformation
Extract data from source systems, apply necessary transformations, and prepare it for loading

• Data Loading
Load transformed data into the target system, ensuring data consistency and accuracy

Testing and Validation

- Unit Testing
Test individual components of data integration processes for functionality.

- Integration Testing
Verify that data flows correctly between systems and that transformations are accurate

- User Acceptance Testing (UAT)
Involve end-users to validate that integrated data meets their requirements.

Monitoring and Maintenance

- Regular Data Audits
Conduct periodic audits to identify and rectify data inconsistencies or errors.

- Performance Monitoring
Monitor system performance to ensure data integration operates efficiently.

- Scalability and Flexibility
Plan for scalability to accommodate growing data volumes and evolving business needs

Access Controls

Implementing access controls and authentication mechanisms to restrict data access based on roles and permissions is a fundamental aspect of information security and data protection.

This practice is crucial for several reasons:

- Data Privacy and Compliance: Many regulatory frameworks, such as the General Data Protection Regulation (GDPR) and the Health Insurance Portability and Accountability Act (HIPAA), require organizations to safeguard sensitive data and ensure that only authorized individuals can access it. Implementing access controls and authentication mechanisms helps companies comply with these regulations and avoid legal consequences.

- Confidentiality: Protecting the confidentiality of sensitive data is paramount. Without proper access controls, unauthorized users can gain access to sensitive information, leading to data breaches, leaks, or theft. Access controls ensure that only those with a legitimate need can view or manipulate data.

- Data Integrity: Unauthorized changes to data can be disastrous, leading to erroneous decisions or compromised business operations. By restricting access based on roles and permissions, organizations can minimize the risk of data tampering and ensure data integrity.

Preventing Insider Threats: Even within an organization, not all employees should have access to all data. Implementing role-based access controls (RBAC) helps avoid threats of insider by limiting employees' access to the data required for their specific job functions. This reduces the likelihood of employees intentionally or unintentionally mishandling data.

- Security Layers: Access controls and authentication mechanisms add layers of security to a system. This multi-layered approach makes it more challenging for attackers to breach a system. Even if an attacker gains access to one level, they may be unable to proceed further without the necessary credentials or permissions.

- Mitigating External Threats: External threats, such as hackers and cybercriminals, are always looking for vulnerabilities to exploit. Implementing strong authentication methods like two-factor authentication (2FA) or multi-factor authentication (MFA) adds an extra layer of defense, making it significantly more difficult for unauthorized individuals to access sensitive data.

- Customization and Flexibility: Access controls and authentication mechanisms allow organizations to customize access based on specific roles, departments, or even individual users. This level of granularity ensures that each user gets the precise level of access required to perform their tasks without unnecessary exposure to sensitive data.

- Auditing and Accountability: These mechanisms also play a crucial role in auditing and accountability. When access to data is controlled and logged, organizations can trace who accessed what data, when, and for what purpose. This information is invaluable for investigating security incidents or compliance audits.

- Scalability: As organizations grow and their workforce evolves, access controls and authentication mechanisms can be easily scaled to accommodate new roles, permissions, and users. This scalability ensures that security measures remain effective as the organization changes.

- Trust and Reputation: Implementing robust access controls and authentication mechanisms helps build trust with customers, partners, and stakeholders. Knowing that their data is secure and protected instills confidence in the organization's ability to handle sensitive information responsibly, which can enhance its reputation.

Implementing access controls and authentication mechanisms to restrict data access based on roles and permissions is essential for safeguarding sensitive data, complying with regulations, preventing breaches, and maintaining trust. It is a foundational element of modern cybersecurity practices and should be a priority for any organization that values data security and privacy.

Leveraging Integrated Data for Results

In today's data-driven business landscape, organizations are increasingly recognizing the importance of leveraging integrated data for achieving optimal results in reporting, analytics, and decision-making. This integrated approach to data management involves the aggregation, consolidation, and harmonization of diverse data sources into a unified platform.

Here's why harnessing this integrated data is essential for various facets of your business:

• Robust Reporting and Analytics:
Integrated data serves as the foundation for robust reporting and analytics. When data from various sources is seamlessly integrated, it eliminates data silos and ensures that all relevant information is readily available for analysis. This results in more accurate, comprehensive, and up-to-date reports and analytics. Robust reporting and analytics enable organizations to track key performance indicators (KPIs), monitor trends, and identify opportunities and challenges. This, in turn, enables informed strategic planning and decision-making.

• Data-Driven Decision Making:
Empowering teams with integrated data accelerates the decision-making process. When employees have easy

access to a unified data repository, they can quickly retrieve the information they need to make informed choices. This agility is particularly valuable in fast-paced industries, allowing organizations to respond swiftly to changing market conditions, customer preferences, and emerging trends. Data-driven decision-making minimizes guesswork and fosters a culture of evidence-based choices, ultimately leading to more efficient operations and better outcomes.

• Customer Insights:

Integrated customer data is a goldmine for understanding your audience and personalizing services. By consolidating data from multiple touchpoints, such as sales, marketing, customer support, and online interactions, you can create a comprehensive customer profile. This profile helps you gain deep insights into customer behavior, preferences, and needs. Armed with this knowledge, you can tailor your products, services, and marketing strategies to individual customers or segments. This personalization enhances the overall customer experience, increases customer loyalty, and drives revenue growth.

• Operational Efficiency:

Integrating data streamlines internal processes. It reduces the time and effort required to gather, clean, and prepare data for reporting and analysis. This, in turn, leads to significant time and cost savings. With integrated data, employees spend less time searching for information and more time using it productively. As a result, organizations become more agile and responsive, optimizing their operations and resource allocation.

• Compliance and Risk Management:

Integrated data aids in compliance and risk management. In regulated industries, maintaining accurate and auditable records is crucial. Integrated data ensures that compliance requirements are met by providing a complete and traceable data trail. Moreover, it enhances risk management by providing a holistic view of potential risks and vulnerabilities, allowing organizations to proactively address issues before they escalate.

Leveraging integrated data for reporting, analytics, and decision-making is a transformative strategy that can empower your organization to thrive in today's competitive business environment. It not only improves the quality and timeliness of information but also enables more strategic and customer-centric decision-making.

By breaking down data silos and harnessing the power of integrated data, you can unlock new opportunities for growth, innovation, and efficiency.

Continuous Improvement

• Feedback Loop
Establish a feedback mechanism to gather input from users and stakeholders for continuous improvement.

• Training and Skill Development
Invest in training to enhance the skills of your data integration team

• Scalability and Growth
Continuously assess and adapt your data integration strategy to support organizational growth

Achieving triumphant data integration is an ever-evolving journey that vitalizes your organization's growth. Embrace these essential steps and best practices to unleash the unbridled power of integrated data, revolutionizing your internal operations and elevating customer experiences to unparalleled heights!

Chapter 6: Comparing Aggregate Data and Surveys: Key Considerations

Making data-driven decisions with aggregate data, rather than sample size data, offers several advantages in the business world. First and foremost, aggregate data provides a comprehensive and holistic view of the entire dataset, ensuring that decisions are based on a complete picture of the situation. This reduces the risk of drawing conclusions from a limited subset of data that may not accurately represent the broader context.

Moreover, aggregate data enhances the reliability and statistical significance of the insights derived from it. With larger sample sizes, the margin of error decreases, making the results more robust and dependable. This is particularly crucial in critical business decisions where accuracy is paramount.

Additionally, aggregate data allows businesses to identify and understand trends, patterns, and outliers more effectively. It enables the detection of subtle nuances that might be missed when working with smaller samples, thereby providing more valuable insights for strategic planning and problem-solving.

Furthermore, aggregate data is often necessary for addressing complex business challenges that involve understanding the behavior of various subgroups or segments within a population. Small sample sizes may not provide sufficient representation of these subsets, leading to erroneous conclusions.

Relying on aggregate data in business decision-making offers greater reliability, accuracy, and the ability to uncover deeper insights. While sample size data can still be useful for preliminary analysis, it's generally more advantageous to base critical decisions on a broader, more comprehensive dataset to ensure the best outcomes for an organization.

There are several reasons why aggregate data is preferable:

- Increased statistical power: Aggregate data includes a larger number of observations, which enhances the statistical power of the analysis. This means that the results are more likely to accurately reflect the true characteristics or patterns of the population being studied.

- Reduced sampling bias: Small survey samples can be prone to sampling bias, where the sample does not adequately represent the population of interest. This can lead to misleading or skewed results. Aggregate data, on the other hand, tends to minimize the impact of sampling bias by including a broader range of individuals or data points.

- Enhanced generalizability: When analyzing aggregate data, the findings are more likely to be generalizable to the larger population. This is particularly important when making decisions or drawing conclusions that apply beyond the specific sample or survey being studied. Aggregate data provides a more comprehensive perspective and reduces the risk of making inaccurate generalizations.

- Improved reliability and stability: Small survey samples are more susceptible to random variations and fluctuations, which can lead to unreliable or inconsistent results. Aggregate data, with its larger sample size, tends to be more stable and less influenced by individual outliers or random variability. This stability increases confidence in the findings and strengthens the reliability of the conclusions drawn.

- Ability to explore subgroups: Aggregate data allows for meaningful analysis of subgroups within the population. With a larger dataset, it becomes possible to examine variations and differences across different demographic groups, geographic regions, or other relevant categories. This can provide valuable insights into disparities, trends, or patterns that might be missed with smaller survey samples.

While small survey samples can still offer valuable insights, they often come with limitations in terms of representativeness and statistical power. By utilizing aggregate data, researchers and analysts can gain a more accurate and comprehensive understanding of the population under study, leading to more robust conclusions and informed decision-making.

Compiled (Aggregate) Data vs. Customer Satisfaction (CSAT) & Net Promoter Score (NPS)

In contemporary business environments, characterized by the extensive accumulation of customer data, encompassing their behaviors, interactions with companies, and more, what are the key advantages of prioritizing the utilization of authentic customer usage data over traditional Customer Satisfaction (CSAT) and Net Promoter Score (NPS) surveys?

1. Objective and Unbiased: Actual customer usage data is objective and doesn't rely on customers' subjective opinions. It reflects what customers are actually doing, not just what they say they're doing.

2. Real-time Insights: Usage data provides real-time insights into customer behavior. This allows businesses to react quickly to changing trends and address issues promptly, whereas CSAT and NPS surveys are typically conducted periodically and may not capture timely feedback.

3. Behavioral Patterns: Actual usage data reveals behavioral patterns and trends that may not be apparent in surveys. It helps identify what features or products customers find most valuable and how they are actually using them.

4. Segmentation and Personalization: Customer usage data can be used to segment customers based on their behavior, allowing for more personalized marketing, product recommendations, and customer experiences. Surveys alone may not provide enough granularity for effective segmentation.

5. Product Improvement: Usage data can inform product development and improvement efforts. It helps businesses understand which features are underutilized or causing problems, leading to data-driven decisions for product enhancements.

6. Cost Efficiency: Collecting usage data is typically more cost-effective than conducting surveys, especially if the customer base is large. Surveys can be resource-intensive, while data collection can often be automated.

7. Reduced Bias: Surveys can suffer from response bias, where respondents may exaggerate their satisfaction or may not provide honest feedback to avoid confrontation. Usage data is less prone to such biases.

8. Holistic Understanding: Actual usage data provides a more holistic understanding of the customer journey, including touchpoints that may not be covered by surveys. This helps in designing end-to-end customer experiences.

9. Benchmarking Competitors: Usage data can be used to benchmark your business against competitors by comparing how customers engage with your products or services versus those of your competitors.

10. Predictive Analytics: Customer usage data can be leveraged for predictive analytics, helping businesses forecast customer behavior, churn, and future trends more accurately. This can be invaluable for proactive decision-making.

11. Longitudinal Analysis: Usage data allows for longitudinal analysis, tracking changes in customer behavior over time. This can help in understanding how customer preferences evolve and adjusting strategies accordingly.
12. Quantifiable Metrics: Usage data provides quantifiable metrics, making it easier to set specific performance targets and measure progress accurately.

While CSAT and NPS surveys have their place in gathering customer feedback, relying solely on them may limit a business's ability to gain deep insights and make data-driven decisions. Actual customer usage data complements survey data by offering a more comprehensive, objective, and actionable view of customer behavior, ultimately leading to more informed business strategies and improved customer experiences.

Section 7

Data Storytelling

Data storytelling is the magical art of turning boring, incomprehensible numbers into riveting tales that will have you on the edge of your seat, clutching your spreadsheet like it's the latest bestseller. Get ready, folks, because we're about to embark on a journey through the thrilling world of data storytelling.

Who needs action-packed movies or gripping novels when you can have bar charts and pie graphs? Am I right? Forget about the adrenaline rush of a car chase or the suspense of a murder mystery – we're diving headfirst into the heart-pounding realm of data visualization. Hold onto your data sets, because things are about to get wild.

But seriously, data storytelling is a pretty useful skill. It's all about taking data and presenting it in a way that's informative and engaging. So, if you're ready to explore the electrifying universe of data storytelling (or at least as electrifying as data can get), buckle up because it will be a wild ride.

***

In today's data-driven world, organizations across the globe are constantly collecting vast amounts of data about their operations, customers, and market trends. This wealth of information has the potential to revolutionize decision-making processes and drive business success.

However, data's sheer volume and complexity can be overwhelming, leaving many organizations struggling to extract meaningful insights. This is where the art of data storytelling comes into play.

Data storytelling is a powerful technique that bridges the gap between raw data and actionable insights. It involves transforming data into a compelling narrative that can be easily understood and interpreted by employees at all levels of an organization.

By harnessing the power of data storytelling, organizations can empower their employees to make informed, data-driven decisions that drive growth and innovation.

This journey towards effective data storytelling is not just about mastering technical skills or deploying the latest data visualization tools. It's about fostering a data-driven culture within your organization, where every employee understands the value of data and feels confident in their ability to use it to drive decisions. This guide will explore the principles and best practices of data storytelling, providing you with the tools and knowledge to embark on this transformative journey.

Whether you're just beginning your data storytelling initiative or looking to enhance your existing practices, this guide will be valuable. By the end of this journey, your organization will be better equipped to harness the power of data storytelling to inform, inspire, and empower your workforce, ultimately leading to more informed and effective decision-making processes across the board. Let's embark on this data-driven adventure together.

This guide will walk you through the key steps to leverage data visualization for your organization as you embark on your journey toward data-driven decision-making.

Step 1: Define Your Objectives

Before you start creating visualizations, clarify your objectives. What decisions are you trying to inform? Who are the key stakeholders? What questions should your data visualizations answer? Establishing clear objectives will guide the entire process.

Step 2: Gather and Prepare Data

Data visualization is only as good as the data it's based on. Ensure data quality, accuracy, and consistency. Clean and preprocess data as needed. Merge and integrate data sources to provide a comprehensive view of the information relevant to your objectives.

Step 3: Choose the Right Visualization Tools

Select appropriate tools for creating your visualizations. Popular options include:

- Data Visualization Libraries: Libraries like D3.js, Matplotlib, and ggplot2 for creating custom visualizations.
- Business Intelligence (BI) Tools: Tools like Tableau, Power BI, and QlikView offer user-friendly interfaces for creating interactive visualizations.
- Programming Languages: Python, R, and JavaScript are common choices for creating custom visualizations.

Choose the tool that aligns with your team's skills and the complexity of your data visualization needs.

Step 4: Design Effective Visualizations

Effective data visualizations should be:

- Clear: Ensure that your visualizations are easy to understand. Use appropriate chart types (e.g., bar charts, line charts, scatter plots) for your data.
- Concise: Eliminate clutter and focus on the most critical information.
- Engaging: Make your visualizations visually appealing to maintain stakeholder interest.
- Interactive: If possible, allow users to interact with the visualizations to explore data on their own.

Step 5: Tell a Story

Data visualizations should tell a story. Create a narrative flow that guides viewers through the data, highlighting key insights and implications. When introducing data visualization to your organization, it's important to use visuals that effectively communicate the value and importance of data visualization.

Here are some good visuals and strategies to leverage:

- Before and After Comparisons:
Show examples of raw data and then visualize the same data to demonstrate how visualization can make complex information more understandable and actionable.

- Impact on Decision-Making:
Display scenarios where data visualization led to better decision-making and outcomes. Share specific success stories or case studies within your organization.

- Inefficiency Illustrations:
Use visuals to represent common inefficiencies, such as lengthy reports, complex spreadsheets, or data overload. Show how data visualization can simplify and streamline these processes.

- Comparison of Visualization Types:
Compare different types of visualizations (e.g., bar charts, line graphs, pie charts) to illustrate how each can be used effectively for different types of data and insights.

- Real-Time Data Dashboards:
Demonstrate the power of real-time data dashboards with live examples showing your organization's current trends or KPIs. Make it interactive if possible.

- Interactive Infographics:
Create interactive infographics that allow employees to explore data visually, encouraging engagement and understanding.

- Data Quality Impact:
Show how data visualization can reveal data quality issues by highlighting inconsistencies or outliers, emphasizing the need for data accuracy.

- Competitor Analysis:
Compare your organization's data visualization practices to those of competitors or industry leaders, highlighting the competitive advantage gained through effective visualization.

- Trends Over Time:
Visualize historical data trends to demonstrate how visualization can reveal insights and patterns that might be missed in tabular data.

- User-Friendly Tools:
Showcase user-friendly data visualization tools or platforms
that your organization can adopt. Provide demonstrations or
tutorials to highlight their ease of use.

- Customization Options:
Emphasize the ability to customize visualizations to
suit specific needs and preferences, showing that
data visualization can be tailored to the organization's
requirements.

- ROI Calculations:
Provide data-driven calculations that show the potential
return on investment (ROI) of implementing data visualization
tools and practices, including time and cost savings.

- Accessibility and Inclusivity:
Highlight the importance of creating accessible visualizations
that individuals with different abilities can understand. Show
examples of accessible design principles.

- Interactive Workshops or Training Sessions:
Offer hands-on workshops or training sessions where
employees can create simple visualizations themselves.
This practical experience can be highly effective.

- Infographics Explaining Benefits:
Use infographics to communicate data visualization's
benefits, such as improved communication, faster insights,
and data-driven decision-making.

- Data Stories:
Share compelling data stories that weave together data,
visuals, and narratives to illustrate how visualization can
communicate complex information effectively.

- Visualization Roadmap:
Present a roadmap for how data visualization will be integrated into the organization's processes and decision-making, demonstrating a clear plan for implementation.

Remember to tailor your approach to your organization's needs, culture, and goals. Clear explanations and discussions should accompany visuals to ensure employees understand data visualization's value and importance.

Step 6: Ensure Accessibility and Responsiveness

Make sure your visualizations are accessible to all users, including those with disabilities. Test visualizations on different devices and screen sizes to ensure responsiveness.

Step 7: Train Your Team

Invest in training for your team to build data visualization skills. Encourage the adoption of best practices and ensure that team members are proficient in using the chosen visualization tools.

Creating a training plan for a team to enhance their data-driven decision-making skills using data visualization outputs is crucial for ensuring that the team can effectively leverage data insights. Below is a comprehensive training plan designed to achieve this goal:

Training Goal: To improve the team's ability to make informed decisions by effectively interpreting and utilizing data visualization outputs.

Phase 1: Interpreting Data Visualizations

Week 1-2: Data Analysis Skills
- Understanding descriptive statistics
- Identifying trends and patterns
- Creating hypotheses from visualizations

Week 3-4: Data-driven Decision Making
- Linking data insights to business objectives
- The role of data in decision-making processes
- Decision-making frameworks and models

Week 5-6: Presenting Findings
- Effective communication of insights
- Storytelling through data
- Handling questions and objections

Phase 2: Practical Application and Projects

Week 1-4: Team Projects and Case Studies
- Divide the team into groups
- Provide real-world datasets and business scenarios
- Each group works on a data-driven project
- Regular reviews and guidance from trainers

Week 5-6: Final Presentation and Certification
- Each group presents their project findings
- Evaluation based on project outcomes
- Certificates awarded to successful participants

Ongoing Support:

- Regular workshops and knowledge-sharing sessions.
- Access to advanced courses or certifications for those who want to specialize.
- Encourage the team to apply their skills on real projects to reinforce learning.

Evaluation:

- Continuous assessment throughout the training.
- Assessment of project outcomes.
- Feedback from team members and trainers

By following this training plan, your team will have a solid foundation in data visualization, data analysis, and data-driven decision-making, enabling them to leverage data effectively to make informed decisions in your organization.

Step 8: Share and Collaborate

Distribute your visualizations to the relevant stakeholders. This can be done through reports, dashboards, or presentations. Encourage collaboration and discussions around the insights derived from the visualizations.

Step 9: Monitor and Iterate

Data-driven decision-making is an ongoing process. Continuously monitor the impact of your visualizations on decision-making processes. Collect feedback from users and iterate on your visualizations to improve their effectiveness.

Step 10: Foster a Data-Driven Culture

Promoting a data-driven culture within your organization is crucial in today's data-centric business landscape. Organizations can gain a competitive edge and make more informed choices by fostering an environment where data is at the core of decision-making processes. Encouraging decision-makers to rely on data and visualizations when making choices is pivotal in this endeavor.

Data-driven decisions are often more accurate and less prone to biases, which can lead to improved outcomes and resource utilization. Providing decision-makers with the tools and training necessary to interpret and utilize data effectively can further empower them to harness the potential of data-driven insights.

Recognition and rewards play a significant role in reinforcing a data-driven culture.

Acknowledging and celebrating data-driven achievements and insights motivates individuals and teams and sets a precedent for others to follow. This recognition can take various forms, such as promotions, bonuses, or public acknowledgment. By linking rewards to data-driven outcomes, organizations clearly communicate their commitment to data excellence. This, in turn, encourages employees at all levels to actively engage with data and seek opportunities to leverage it for improved decision-making.

Building a data-driven culture within your organization is about implementing the right tools and technologies and fostering a mindset that values data as a strategic asset. By encouraging decision-makers to base their choices on data and reinforcing this behavior through recognition and rewards, organizations can unlock the full potential of their data, driving innovation, efficiency, and competitiveness in today's dynamic business environment.

Data visualization is a powerful tool for organizations committed to data-driven decision-making. Following these steps and continuously refining your approach can transform data into actionable insights that drive your organization's success. Embracing data visualization as a core element of your data strategy will empower your team to make informed decisions and stay competitive in today's data-rich world.

Section 8

Data-Driven Employee Support:
Maximizing Your Team's
Potential w/ Statistics + Data

Welcome to the magical world of Statistics and data-driven Employee Support! If you thought statistics were just a snooze-fest of numbers and data was something only your computer geek cousin cared about, think again. We're about to embark on a thrilling journey to explore the exhilarating highs and gut-wrenching lows of supporting employees through the power of...drumroll, please... statistics!

Yes, it's true. In this wild ride, we'll take you through the riveting world of pie charts, bar graphs, and scatter plots. Forget those boring conversations with your coworkers at the water cooler; now, you can dazzle them with your newfound knowledge of standard deviations and correlation coefficients. Who needs friends when you have statistics? Am I right?

But wait, there's more! We'll also show you how to use data to make informed decisions about employee support. Because who needs intuition or common sense when you can rely on data to tell you what to do? After all, why trust your gut when you can trust a spreadsheet?

So, fasten your seatbelts, dear readers, because we're about to dive headfirst into the thrilling, pulse-pounding world of Statistics and data-driven Employee Support. You'll laugh and cry, and you might even learn something along the way (though we can't make any promises).

Get ready for a rollercoaster of epic proportions because data has never been this exhilarating!

***

In today's fast-paced and highly competitive business landscape, organizations must harness the power of data to stay ahead of the curve. One area where data-driven insights can significantly impact is employee support and development. By leveraging statistics and data analytics, companies can unlock the full potential of their teams, leading to increased productivity, job satisfaction, and, ultimately, greater success.

The Power of Data in Employee Support

Data Driven employee support isn't just a trend; it's a necessity for modern businesses. It involves collecting, analyzing, and interpreting data to make informed decisions about supporting and developing your workforce. This approach enables organizations to move away from one-size-fits-all solutions and tailor their support strategies to individual employee needs.

Here are some key ways in which data-driven employee support can transform your organization:

Personalized Development Plans

One of the most significant advantages of using data in employee support is the ability to create personalized development plans. Organizations can design training programs and growth opportunities that align with their unique strengths and weaknesses by analyzing an employee's performance data, feedback, and career goals. This personalized approach boosts individual performance and fosters a sense of value and belonging among employees.

Predictive Analytics for Talent Retention

High employee turnover is costly and disruptive to business operations. Data analytics can help predict which employees are at risk of leaving and why. By identifying these patterns early on, organizations can take proactive measures to retain valuable talent. This might include offering career advancement opportunities, addressing workplace concerns, or providing additional training.

Performance Evaluation and Feedback

Gone are the days of annual performance reviews as the sole source of employee feedback. Data-driven employee support allows for continuous performance monitoring. Managers can provide real-time feedback, and employees can access dashboards displaying their performance metrics. This regular feedback loop promotes ongoing improvement and ensures employees align with organizational goals.

Skill Gap Analysis

In rapidly evolving industries, skill gaps can hinder a company's progress. Data Driven analysis of employee skills can identify areas where training or upskilling is needed. This ensures that employees remain competitive in their roles and can adapt to changing job requirements.

Implementing DataDriven Employee Support

To harness the full potential of data-driven employee support, organizations must follow a structured approach:

1. Data Collection

Start by gathering relevant data from various sources

within your organization. This could include performance metrics, employee surveys, feedback, and even external data sources such as industry benchmarks. Ensure data collection is consistent, accurate, and compliant with privacy regulations.

2. Data Analysis

Use statistical methods and data analytics tools to analyze the collected data. Identify trends, correlations, and insights that can inform your employee support strategies. For example, you might discover that employees who receive regular training are more engaged and productive.

3. Designing Support Programs

Based on your data analysis, design tailored employee support programs. These could include mentoring, coaching, skills training, or wellness initiatives. Ensure that these programs are flexible and adaptable to accommodate individual employee needs.

4. Continuous Monitoring

Implement a system for continuous monitoring and evaluation. Regularly assess the effectiveness of your support programs by tracking key performance indicators and gathering employee feedback. Use this information to make data-driven adjustments as needed.

5. Data Privacy and Security

Protect employee data rigorously. Ensure that your data storage and processing practices comply with relevant privacy laws and regulations, such as GDPR or HIPAA, depending on your jurisdiction and industry.

Case Study: SDSS Corp.

Let's look at how SDSS Corp., a fictitious company, embraced data-driven employee support:

Step 1: Data Collection
SDSS Corp. implemented an employee portal where data on performance, goals, training history, and feedback were regularly updated. This allowed for a comprehensive view of each employee's development journey.

Step 2: Data Analysis
The HR team at SDSS Corp. employed data analytics tools to identify patterns in employee performance and feedback. They discovered that employees who received Success Sponsorship were more likely to achieve their career goals.

Step 3: Designing Support Programs
In response to their findings, SDSS Corp. launched a Success Sponsorship program, matching experienced employees with those seeking career growth. The flexible program allowed employees to choose mentors based on their specific career aspirations.

Step 4: Continuous Monitoring
Regular surveys and performance data analysis helped

SDSS Corp. track the program's success. Over time, they saw increased job satisfaction and performance among employees who participated in the Success Sponsorship program.

Step 5: Data Privacy and Security
SDSS Corp. took data privacy seriously, implementing stringent security measures to protect employee data. They maintained compliance with all relevant regulations, earning trust among their workforce.

Organizations must leverage statistics and data analytics to maximize their team's potential in the data-driven era. Employee support strategies that are based on data-driven insights not only increase productivity but also lead to a more engaged and satisfied workforce. By embracing this approach, your organization can stay ahead of the competition and thrive in today's ever-evolving business landscape.

Chapter 1: Tech + Talent

In the fast-paced world of modern workplaces, understanding your employees' well-being and behavior is crucial. One powerful AI tool for achieving this understanding is Natural Language Understanding (NLU) and Natural Language Processing (NLP) applications. These technologies enable organizations to review sentiment, rate of speech, tone, voice inflection, and vocabulary changes in employee communications, which can be invaluable in identifying behavioral changes.

In this chapter, we'll explore how NLU and NLP applications can help organizations detect and address shifts in employee behavior.

The Role of NLU & NLP in Employee Behavior Analysis

NLU and NLP applications are designed to analyze and interpret human language. They can process vast amounts of text and spoken communication, providing insights into employee sentiment, communication style, and emotional states. Here's how these technologies can be instrumental in identifying behavior changes:

Sentiment Analysis

Sentiment analysis tools can assess the emotional tone of written or spoken communication. Organizations can identify sentiment changes over time by analyzing emails, chat messages, or even voice recordings. A sudden shift from positive to negative sentiment may indicate an issue that needs attention, such as increased stress or dissatisfaction.

Rate of Speech

NLP algorithms can measure the rate employees speak during meetings, presentations, or recorded conversations. Significant variations in speech rate, such as rapid speech or prolonged pauses, can signal changes in confidence, nervousness, or potential stressors. This information can be especially valuable in assessing employees' mental and emotional well-being.

Tone and Voice Inflection

NLU applications can analyze the tone and voice inflection in written or spoken words. Changes in tone, such as becoming more aggressive, defensive, or subdued, can indicate shifts in attitude, emotions, or interpersonal dynamics. Detecting these changes early can help organizations address underlying issues promptly.

Vocabulary Changes

NLP models can track vocabulary changes in written communication & transcribed voice audio files. An employee who suddenly starts using more negative or critical language may be experiencing frustration or dissatisfaction.

Conversely, an increase in positive language might indicate improved morale or engagement. A sudden change in vocabulary might also signal that an employee is experiencing increased stress or emotional exhaustion, which can impact their job performance and well-being.

Practical Applications in the Workplace

Implementing NLU and NLP applications for employee behavior analysis requires careful planning and ethical considerations. Here are some practical applications:

• Employee Well-being Monitoring
By regularly analyzing employee emails, chat messages, recorded meetings, or transcribed customer voice calls, organizations can gain insights into the emotional well-being of their staff. Unusual sentiment patterns or significant changes in tone can trigger HR interventions to support employees in times of stress or personal challenges.

• Conflict Resolution
NLU and NLP tools can be used to identify escalating conflicts within teams. Changes in tone and increased use of confrontational language can be detected early, allowing for timely intervention to mediate and resolve issues before they become unmanageable.

- Performance Evaluation

In addition to traditional performance metrics, organizations can use NLP to evaluate how employees communicate about their work. Consistently negative language or a lack of engagement in discussions related to work projects may warrant performance reviews and targeted coaching.

- Training and Development

NLP can help customize training and development programs by identifying specific language patterns and communication styles that need improvement. Tailored coaching can be more effective in addressing individual employee needs.

- Diversity and Inclusion

NLU and NLP applications can assist in identifying potential instances of bias or discrimination in workplace communications. This enables organizations to proactively address diversity and inclusion issues and promote a more equitable work environment.

Ethical Considerations and Privacy

While NLU and NLP applications offer valuable insights, addressing ethical concerns and respecting employee privacy is essential. Organizations must communicate their data collection and analysis practices, obtain consent when necessary, and implement strict data security measures to protect employee information.

NLU and NLP applications have revolutionized how organizations understand and respond to employee behavior changes. By leveraging these technologies, businesses can create a more supportive and inclusive workplace, improve employee well-being, and enhance productivity. However, it is crucial to approach the implementation of these tools with a commitment to privacy and ethical considerations, ensuring that employee trust and privacy are maintained throughout the process.

✸ Chapter 2: Process Behavior Charts (Standard Deviation)

The empirical rule, also known as the 689599.7 rule or the three-sigma rule, is a statistical guideline describing the approximate data distribution in a bell-shaped or normal distribution curve. This rule is particularly useful in understanding how data is distributed in many real-world situations.

Here's a breakdown of the empirical rule:

- 68% Rule: According to the empirical rule, approximately 68% of the data in a normal distribution falls within one standard deviation of the mean (average) in both directions. In other words, about 68% of the data points are within one standard deviation above the mean and one below the mean.

- 95% Rule: Approximately 95% of the data falls within two standard deviations of the mean. This means most data points (about 95%) are within two standard deviations above the mean and two standard deviations below the mean in a normal distribution.

- 99.7% Rule: The empirical rule states that roughly 99.7% of the data falls within three standard deviations of the mean. This implies that almost all data points (about 99.7%) are within three standard deviations above the mean and three standard deviations below the mean in a normal distribution.

In a visual representation, if you were to draw a bell-shaped curve to represent your data, you would find that most data points cluster near the mean, and the further you move away from the mean, the fewer data points you encounter.

The empirical rule is a valuable guideline for understanding data variability and trends.

Using standard deviation as a metric to identify employees needing help can make sense in certain contexts. Standard deviation is a statistical measure that quantifies the variation or dispersion within a dataset. In the case of employee performance or well-being, standard deviation can help identify individuals who deviate significantly from the average or norm.

Here are a few reasons why using standard deviation to identify employees who need help can be meaningful:

Outliers Detection

In the ever-evolving landscape of modern businesses, optimizing employee performance is crucial to achieving success. To this end, organizations rely on various tools and techniques to monitor and enhance their workforce's productivity and efficiency. One valuable method for identifying exceptional cases is using standard deviation to detect outliers in employee performance.

Understanding Outliers

Before delving into how standard deviation can help unearth outliers in the context of employee performance, let's clearly understand what outliers are and why they matter. Outliers are data points that significantly deviate from the average or mean of a dataset.

These anomalies can emerge for various reasons, such as errors in data collection, exceptional circumstances, or genuine differences in performance. In human resources and employee management, outliers can manifest as individuals performing exceptionally well or significantly below the average level.

The Power of Standard Deviation

Standard deviation, a statistical measure, is valuable for identifying outliers within a dataset. It quantifies the amount of variation or dispersion present in a data set. In the context of employee performance, standard deviation can be an invaluable ally in the quest to pinpoint employees who are exceptional or who may be struggling.

Setting the Threshold

Establishing an appropriate threshold is the first step in using standard deviation for outlier detection in employee performance. This threshold is a yardstick defining what constitutes a significant deviation from the average. By setting this threshold judiciously, organizations can distinguish between employees who warrant attention and those performing within the expected range.

Identifying High Performers

When employees consistently achieve performance metrics well above the mean, they can be considered high performers or outliers. These individuals drive an organization's success and can serve as role models for others. Identifying high performers is essential for recognizing their contributions and leveraging their expertise to elevate the entire team's performance.

Standard deviation can help pinpoint these exceptional employees by highlighting their consistent performance above the established threshold. Managers and HR professionals can then implement strategies to retain and nurture these high-performing individuals, ensuring they continue to excel.

Identifying Strugglers

Conversely, standard deviation can help organizations identify employees who consistently perform below the mean. These individuals may face challenges affecting their work or require additional support and training. Identifying strugglers early is vital to prevent performance issues from escalating and affecting the overall team's productivity. By setting a threshold below the mean with standard deviation, organizations can identify these struggling employees and offer them the necessary assistance through additional training, Success Sponsorship, or addressing underlying issues hindering their performance.

Performance Assessment

Standard deviation can provide insights into the distribution of performance within a team or organization. If there are employees with high levels of performance variability (high standard deviation), it may indicate inconsistent performance or potential issues that require attention. Identifying these individuals can help allocate resources to improve their performance or address underlying concerns.

Well-Being Monitoring

Standard deviation can also be used to assess employees' well-being or job satisfaction. By analyzing factors such as absenteeism, productivity, or survey responses, you can calculate the standard deviation to understand the variation in well-being across the workforce. Employees with significantly low or high well-being scores (beyond a certain standard deviation) may need additional support or interventions.

Monitoring Well-Being through Standard Deviation

Well-being is a multifaceted aspect of an individual's life that encompasses physical, mental, and emotional health and overall satisfaction with life. In both personal and organizational contexts, monitoring well-being has become crucial to maintaining a healthy and productive workforce.

Standard deviation can be a valuable tool in this endeavor, helping to assess and manage well-being effectively.

Measuring Well-Being

Well-being is often assessed using various metrics and surveys, which capture stress levels, job satisfaction, work-life balance, and physical health data. These metrics are essential for understanding individuals' overall health and happiness and can provide valuable insights for organizations aiming to create a supportive and thriving environment.

Utilizing Standard Deviation

Standard deviation can be a valuable statistical measure when monitoring well-being because it allows organizations to identify the extent of variation within well-being metrics across a group of individuals.

Here's how standard deviation can be applied to well-being monitoring:

• Identifying High Variability
A high standard deviation in well-being metrics indicates a significant variation among individuals within a group. This could mean that some employees are experiencing substantially higher levels of well-being than others. Identifying this variation is crucial because it suggests that well-being support strategies may need to be tailored to address the diverse needs of employees.

• Targeting Intervention
Using standard deviation as a guide, organizations can pinpoint employees experiencing well-being levels significantly lower or higher than the group's average. Those with notably low well-being may be at risk of burnout, decreased productivity, and even health issues. Conversely, individuals with exceptionally high well-being can exemplify what a healthy work-life balance and a supportive work environment can achieve.

• Assessing the Impact of Well-being Initiatives
When organizations implement well-being improvement initiatives, the standard deviation can be used to measure their effectiveness. A reduction in the standard deviation of well-being metrics over time indicates that the initiatives contribute to a more consistent level of well-being across the organization. This can validate the impact of well-being programs and guide future investments in employee support and wellness initiatives.

- Identifying Trends and Patterns

Regular monitoring of well-being metrics and their standard deviations can help identify organizational trends and patterns. For example, suppose the standard deviation of stress levels is consistently high during certain periods, such as the end of the fiscal year. In that case, organizations can proactively implement stress reduction programs or provide additional support during those times.

Organizations can identify outliers and target their interventions more effectively by analyzing the variation in well-being metrics across a group of individuals. This approach helps employees maintain their health and happiness and contributes to a more productive and engaged workforce.

Early Intervention

Identifying employees who deviate significantly from the norm through standard deviation analysis allows for early intervention. By promptly recognizing potential issues or areas of concern, employers can provide targeted support, training, or resources to help those employees overcome challenges and improve their performance or well-being.

This practice can be applied not only to key performance indicators (KPIs) but to look for patterns, trends, deviations, etc., in data generated by employees that could help identify areas of opportunity to build closer relationships with individuals that strengthen the bond with teammates, reduce attrition and allow for preventive measures or interventions to initiatives, thee highly probably events (employee attrition, sales conversions, first contact resolution, etc.

Section 9

Teaching Employees How To Use Data

In the contemporary business milieu dominated by data, the capacity to discern actionable insights and formulate well-informed decisions through data analysis has transcended the realm of mere competence; it has become an unmistakable imperative.

As a reservoir of potential knowledge, data is key to unlocking concealed revelations, latent trends, and unexplored opportunities that might otherwise elude detection.

Within the confines of this chapter, we shall embark on a comprehensive exploration of the methodologies and approaches requisite for instilling in employees the acumen to grasp the intricacies of data and the proficiency to discern underlying patterns therein.

Our overarching goal is to empower individuals with the analytical prowess necessary to drive superior business outcomes through data-driven decision-making.

The Importance of Data Literacy

Data literacy is the foundation upon which effective data-driven decision-making rests. Without it, employees may struggle to interpret data correctly, leading to poor decisions, missed opportunities, and costly mistakes.

Data literacy encompasses several key skills, including:

- Data Collection: It is fundamental to understand where data comes from, how it's gathered, and its reliability. Employees should be aware of data sources, whether they are internal databases, external datasets, or customer feedback.

- Data Analysis: The ability to analyze data involves techniques such as statistical analysis, data visualization, and data modeling. Employees should be able to use tools like Excel, data analytics software, and programming languages like Python or R.

- Data Interpretation: This skill involves making sense of data in the business context. Employees should be able to identify trends, correlations, and outliers that can inform decision-making.

- Data Communication: Being able to convey data insights effectively is crucial. Employees should know how to create clear and compelling data visualizations and reports that facilitate understanding among their peers and superiors.

Chapter 1: Building Data Literacy in Your Team

To teach employees how to understand data and recognize patterns effectively, follow these steps:

Assess Current Data Literacy Levels

To embark on the journey of enhancing your team's data literacy, it is essential to commence with a thorough understanding of your team's current standing in this domain. Initiating this process involves conducting a comprehensive skills assessment or a meticulously crafted survey. The primary objective here is to assiduously pinpoint knowledge gaps and areas that necessitate substantial improvement within your team's data literacy skill set. This initial diagnostic step is a pivotal foundation for your subsequent actions, enabling you to tailor your training and development endeavors to align with your team members' needs and aspirations.

Practically, the skills assessment or survey should be designed thoughtfully. It should encompass a wide spectrum of data-related competencies, encompassing technical skills, an understanding of data concepts, analytical thinking, and the ability to communicate insights effectively. Moreover, it should be structured to encourage honest self-assessment while allowing team members to express their perceptions of the team's overall data literacy status.

Once the data from the assessment or survey is collected and analyzed, a clearer picture of the strengths and weaknesses of your team's data literacy will emerge. This newfound awareness can be instrumental in formulating a tailored and strategic approach to improve data literacy across the team. It allows you to allocate resources efficiently, focusing on areas that demand immediate attention and ensuring that the training efforts are relevant and engaging for team members.

The path to elevating your team's data literacy begins with carefully assessing their current standing and identifying specific knowledge gaps and areas for improvement. This proactive approach empowers you to create a well-informed and targeted strategy that can maximize the effectiveness of your training efforts, ultimately leading to a more data-literate and proficient team capable of harnessing data for better decision-making and problem-solving.

Provide Training and Resources

Allocate resources to invest in diverse training initiatives, encompassing tailored programs and workshops designed to accommodate various skill levels within your team. Deliberate upon the possibility of providing both in-house and externally sourced training alternatives to ensure comprehensive skill development.

 Highly regarded educational resources that warrant exploration encompass a spectrum of options, such as online courses, literature, webinars, and on-demand tutorials. This multifaceted approach will empower your team to attain proficiency and excellence in their respective areas of expertise.

Step 1: Identify Training Needs

In pursuing organizational success, it is imperative to meticulously align your workforce's skills and knowledge with your company's overarching strategic objectives and growth aspirations.

This strategic alignment ensures that your business remains competitive and adaptable and empowers your employees to contribute effectively towards realizing these objectives. It becomes crucial to discern the specific proficiencies and knowledge domains that directly correlate with your company's strategic vision to accomplish this alignment.

By systematically identifying the skills and knowledge areas that harmonize with your business goals, you equip your team with the tools and competencies to propel your company toward its desired outcomes. This approach enhances individual job performance and fosters a collective synergy within your organization, allowing for more streamlined and focused efforts in achieving strategic milestones.

By fostering this alignment, your company can adapt more swiftly to evolving market dynamics, seize emerging opportunities, and effectively mitigate risks. It also provides a clear roadmap for talent acquisition, development, and retention strategies, ensuring that your workforce remains well-equipped to meet the evolving demands of your industry.

Step 2: Develop a Training Plan

- Create a Training Calendar: Develop a calendar outlining yearly training programs and workshops. This calendar should consider the availability and preferences of team members.

- Diversify Training Options: Offer a mix of in-house and external training options. This can include:

- In-House Workshops: Organize workshops conducted by internal experts or external trainers to address specific skill gaps

- Online Courses: Subscribe to online learning platforms or purchase licenses for relevant courses that team members can access at their own pace

- Books and Learning Materials: Provide access to books, ebooks, and learning materials that team members can use to self-study

- Webinars: Host regular webinars on trending industry topics and skills

- On-Demand Tutorials: Create a repository of on-demand tutorials and resources that team members can access when needed

Step 3: Allocate Budget and Resources

Budget Allocation: Determine the budget required for training programs and resources. Ensure it is in line with the company's financial capabilities.

- Resource Allocation: Appoint a training coordinator or team responsible for organizing and overseeing training initiatives.

- Execute Training Programs

- Communication: Inform team members about the training opportunities available to them. Highlight the benefits of skill development for their career growth.

- Enrollment and Registration: Establish a process for team members to enroll in training programs and track their progress.

- Feedback Mechanism: Collect feedback after each training session to assess its effectiveness and make improvements for future programs.

Step 4: Measure and Evaluate

- Skill Assessment Post-Training: After each training program, assess the improvement in team members' skills and knowledge through tests, evaluations, or practical assessments.

- ROI Analysis: Evaluate the return on investment (ROI) by comparing the cost of training to the improved performance and productivity of team members.

Step 5: Continuous Improvement

- Iterate Training Plan: Regularly review and update the training calendar and offerings based on evolving business needs and feedback.

- Promote a Learning Culture: Encourage continuous learning within the organization. Recognize and reward employees who actively participate in training and demonstrate improved skills.

Step 6: Reporting and Documentation

- Maintain Records: Keep detailed records of training programs, attendance, feedback, and skill assessments for reference and reporting purposes.

- Share Success Stories: Share success stories of team members who have benefited from training programs to motivate others.

By following this action plan, you will create a structured and effective approach to investing in training programs, workshops, and resources for your team, ultimately fostering skill development and contributing to the overall success of your organization.

HandsOn Practice

Embracing experiential learning is widely acknowledged as a highly productive approach to cultivating data literacy within your workforce. Rather than merely imparting theoretical knowledge, fostering an environment encouraging employees to actively apply their acquired skills and insights to tangible, real-world situations within your organization can yield profound results.
This entails empowering your team to engage in hands-on data analysis exercises, focusing on practical applications in sales data evaluation, customer behavior analysis, and optimizing operational processes.

Experiential learning catalyzes a more profound comprehension of the subject matter in data literacy. Encouraging your employees to roll up their sleeves and grapple with actual data scenarios solidifies their understanding of data concepts and equips them with invaluable problem-solving skills.

 By enabling your workforce to directly interact with data in their daily work, they become adept at deciphering patterns, extracting meaningful insights, and making data-driven decisions.

The practice of real-world data analysis fosters a deeper appreciation for the significance of data quality and accuracy. Employees realize that the quality of their input data profoundly impacts the reliability of their analyses, thereby instilling a sense of responsibility for maintaining data integrity.

Integrating data literacy into everyday tasks and projects creates a seamless bridge between theory and practice, making learning more engaging and relevant. This approach empowers your employees with a newfound skill set and cultivates a culture of data-driven decision-making throughout your organization.

Promoting experiential learning in data literacy represents a strategic investment in your workforce's capabilities. By encouraging your employees to immerse themselves in practical data applications within your organizational context, you pave the way for a more proficient and data-savvy team, ultimately driving innovation and efficiency in your operations.

Success Sponsorship and Collaboration

A highly effective strategy for fostering a culture of data proficiency within your organization is to strategically pair less experienced team members with their counterparts possessing robust data skills. This initiative, often called "Success Sponsorship," represents a deliberate effort to expedite the learning curve while simultaneously nurturing a collaborative atmosphere where knowledge sharing becomes a cornerstone of professional development.

Success Sponsorship, as a concept, transcends traditional mentorship or apprenticeship models by emphasizing not only the transfer of knowledge but also the facilitation of real-world learning experiences. By connecting less experienced team members with their more data-savvy peers, you orchestrate a symbiotic relationship wherein both parties stand to benefit.

For the less experienced members, this arrangement offers a unique opportunity to glean insights, techniques, and best practices directly from their seasoned counterparts. It allows them to navigate the intricacies of data analysis, interpretation, and application under the guidance of those who have already trodden similar paths.

This not only accelerates their learning but also instills a sense of confidence and competence in handling data-driven tasks.

Conversely, those with advanced data skills find themselves in a position of mentorship and leadership entrusted with imparting their knowledge and expertise. This role encourages them to articulate their methodologies, refine their communication skills, and deepen their understanding of data concepts as they explain them to others. In essence, they become champions of knowledge dissemination within the organization.

Beyond the immediate benefits of skill transfer, Success Sponsorship cultivates a collaborative ecosystem where cross-functional teamwork and mutual support flourish. It fosters an environment where employees can ask questions, seek assistance, and collaborate on data-related projects. This enriches the collective knowledge base and fuels a sense of camaraderie and shared purpose among team members.

Success Sponsorship is a potent mechanism for promoting data literacy and building a culture of collaboration within your organization. By pairing less experienced team members with data-savvy colleagues, you facilitate a dynamic exchange of expertise and experiences, ultimately enhancing the proficiency of your entire workforce while fortifying the bonds of teamwork and mutual growth.

Continuous Learning

Data and technology are at the forefront of innovation and progress in today's rapidly changing landscape. Organizations must prioritize continuous team learning and growth to keep pace with this ever-evolving terrain. The key to staying competitive and relevant is fostering a culture of ongoing education and knowledge sharing.

The dynamism of data and technology mandates that professionals within an organization remain agile in their skill sets and well-versed in the latest tools and techniques. Therefore, as a leader, it is essential to encourage and support your team in their quest for knowledge. This ensures individual development and cultivates a collective mindset that champions progress and innovation.

One of the most effective strategies to facilitate ongoing learning is to offer various learning opportunities. This can include formal training sessions, workshops, webinars, conferences, and access to online courses. Providing a range of options enables your team to tailor their learning experiences to their specific needs and preferences. This approach empowers individuals and reflects a commitment to their professional growth.

Establishing a knowledge-sharing culture within your organization is a powerful way to harness the collective intelligence of your team. Encourage your employees to regularly share interesting insights and findings with their colleagues. This could include weekly knowledge-sharing sessions, internal blogs, or encouraging open discussions during team meetings. By creating a safe and open platform for sharing, you foster an environment where information flows freely, fostering creativity and collaboration.

Consider implementing mentorship programs where experienced team members can guide and support those eager to learn and grow. Mentoring not only accelerates skill development but also strengthens interpersonal connections within the team, fostering a sense of belonging and camaraderie.

In addition to formalized learning opportunities and knowledge sharing, staying updated with the latest trends and technologies should be embedded in your team's daily routine. Encourage team members to follow industry blogs, subscribe to relevant newsletters, and participate in online communities where professionals discuss emerging trends and best practices.

As a leader, you can set an example by prioritizing your continuous learning journey and openly sharing your insights and discoveries with your team. Leading by example demonstrates your commitment to personal growth and inspires your team to follow suit.

An organization's success hinges on its ability to adapt and innovate. By offering ongoing learning opportunities, fostering a culture of knowledge sharing, and championing a commitment to growth, you empower your team to thrive in this dynamic landscape, ultimately ensuring your organization's long-term success and competitiveness.

Feedback and Recognition

Recognizing and rewarding employees demonstrating remarkable progress in their data literacy journey is a powerful practice and a strategic investment in the organization's data-driven future. Data literacy, the ability to interpret, analyze, and derive insights from data, has become a critical skill in today's data-centric business landscape.

Acknowledging and incentivizing employees in this domain enhances their individual growth and fosters a culture of continuous learning and data-driven decision-making within the organization.

- Strategic Importance of Data Literacy:
Data is the lifeblood of modern businesses, and those who can harness its power have a competitive edge. By acknowledging employees who make strides in their data literacy journey, organizations signal the strategic importance of this skill. It communicates that data is not just a resource but a driver of success, and employees who excel in this area are valued contributors.

- Motivation Through Recognition:
Recognizing employees' efforts and achievements in data literacy is a potent motivational tool. It validates their hard work and dedication, boosting their morale and job satisfaction. When employees feel appreciated for their data literacy skills, they are more likely to continue improving and exploring new ways to contribute to the organization's success.

- Inspiring Others to Follow Suit:
The act of acknowledging and rewarding employees for their data literacy journey creates a ripple effect throughout the organization. Others are inspired to embark on their data literacy journey, knowing their efforts will not go unnoticed. It fosters a culture of learning and collaboration, where employees are encouraged to share knowledge and best practices, further enhancing the overall data literacy of the organization.

- Constructive Feedback for Continuous Growth:
While recognition is important, providing constructive feedback to employees on their data literacy journey is equally crucial. Feedback helps them understand their strengths and areas for improvement, guiding them toward becoming more proficient in data analysis and interpretation. Constructive feedback should be specific, actionable, and supportive, encouraging employees to refine their skills continually.

- Tailored Rewards and Incentives:

Rewards and incentives should be tailored to align with the level of achievement in data literacy. This can range from public recognition during team meetings to financial incentives or opportunities for career advancement. By customizing rewards, organizations can ensure employees are motivated and feel appreciated according to their aspirations and goals.

- Building a Data-Driven Culture:

Acknowledging and rewarding data literacy achievements creates a data-driven culture within the organization. Such a culture prioritizes data as a primary resource for decision-making and encourages employees to approach challenges with data-driven solutions. This, in turn, leads to more informed decisions, improved processes, and better business outcomes.

Recognizing and rewarding employees who make significant strides in their data literacy journey is a multifaceted strategy that benefits both individuals and the organization. It motivates and inspires others and reinforces the importance of data in driving business success. By providing constructive feedback and tailored incentives, organizations can cultivate a data-savvy workforce that continually adds value through data-driven insights and decision-making.

⊕ Chapter 2: Recognizing Patterns for Better Business Decision Making

Recognizing patterns in data is an essential aspect of data literacy. Here are some key points to emphasize when teaching your employees about pattern recognition:

1. Start Simple: Begin with patterns like trends (upward or downward movement) and seasonality (recurring patterns). As employees become comfortable with these, they move on to more complex patterns like correlations and anomalies.

2. Visualization Tools: Utilize data visualization tools to make patterns more apparent. Bar charts, line graphs, scatter plots, and heat maps can help employees see trends and relationships more clearly.

3. Context Matters: Remind your team that patterns should always be considered in the business context. Not all patterns are relevant or actionable, so they should be able to differentiate between noise and meaningful insights.

4. HypothesisDriven Analysis: Encourage employees to form hypotheses about the data before diving in. This will help them focus their analysis and look for patterns that might confirm or refute their assumptions.

5. Iterate and Refine: Data analysis is an iterative process. Encourage employees to revisit their analyses regularly, especially when new data becomes available. Patterns may change over time.

Creating a plan to teach and improve employees' skills in recognizing patterns in data requires a systematic and structured approach. Here is a step-by-step plan to achieve this goal:

Step 1: Identify Learning Objectives

Define clear and specific learning objectives that outline what you want employees to achieve. These objectives should be aligned with the organization's goals and the role of data pattern recognition in decision-making.

Example Learning Objectives:

- Understand the significance of data pattern recognition in business.
- Identify common types of patterns in data, such as trends, seasonality, and anomalies.
- Apply data visualization techniques to make patterns in data more apparent.
- Formulate hypotheses and test them through data analysis.
- Interpret and communicate insights derived from pattern recognition effectively.

Step 2: Assess Current Skill Levels

Conduct a skills assessment to gauge employees' current abilities in data pattern recognition. This can be done through surveys, quizzes, or practical exercises. The assessment will help you tailor the training program to address specific knowledge gaps.

Assessing your employees' skill levels in pattern recognition is crucial to effectively tailor training programs and identify improvement areas. Here are various methods you can use to assess their skills:

- Self-Assessment Questionnaires: Provide employees with self-assessment questionnaires or surveys that ask them to rate their proficiency in pattern recognition. This can serve as a baseline and help individuals reflect on their abilities. However, self-assessments may not always be entirely accurate.

Practical Exercises: Create real-world scenarios or case studies where employees must apply their pattern recognition skills. Observe their performance in identifying, interpreting, and communicating patterns from data.

- Written Tests: Develop written tests or quizzes that assess employees' theoretical knowledge of pattern recognition concepts, such as types of patterns (e.g., trends, seasonality), data visualization techniques, and hypothesis-driven analysis.

- Data Analysis Projects: Assign employees projects requiring them to analyze data sets and identify patterns. Evaluate their ability to select appropriate tools and techniques, formulate hypotheses, and draw meaningful conclusions.

- Peer Reviews: Encourage employees to review and provide feedback on each other's data analysis and visualization work. Peer assessments can offer valuable insights into skill levels and areas of improvement.

- Managerial Assessments: Managers and supervisors can provide assessments based on their observations of employees' performance in data-related tasks, their ability to make data-informed decisions, and their overall contributions to the organization.

- Certifications and Qualifications: Consider using external certifications or qualifications as a benchmark for assessing employees' pattern recognition skills. Certifications like Microsoft Certified Data Analyst or Google Data Analytics Certificate can be used to validate their knowledge and skills.

- Data Analytics Software Proficiency: If your organization uses specific data analytics software (e.g., Excel, Tableau, Python, R), you can assess employees' proficiency in using these tools through practical assessments or standardized tests provided by the software vendors.

- Portfolio Review: Encourage employees to maintain a data analysis and visualization project portfolio. Regularly review their portfolios to assess their progression and the quality of their work.

- Continuous Feedback: Foster a culture of continuous feedback, where employees regularly discuss their progress, challenges, and goals with their managers or mentors. This ongoing dialogue can provide valuable insights into skill development.

- Objective Metrics: Establish key performance indicators (KPIs) for pattern recognition and data analysis. Measure employees' performance against these metrics, such as the accuracy of predictions or the effectiveness of data-driven decisions.

- Observation and RolePlaying: Observe employees as they work on data-related tasks or conduct role-playing exercises to simulate real-world scenarios. This can help evaluate their practical application of pattern recognition skills.

- External Assessments: Hire external experts or consultants to evaluate employees' pattern recognition skills through assessments, interviews, or work audits.

- Feedback from Stakeholders: Collect feedback from stakeholders who work closely with employees, such as clients, customers, or other departments. Assess whether employees' data-driven insights have positively impacted business outcomes.

It's often beneficial to use a combination of these assessment methods to comprehensively understand employees' pattern recognition skills.

Additionally, assessments should be conducted periodically to track skill development over time and adjust training and development efforts accordingly.

Step 3: Develop a Curriculum

Design a comprehensive curriculum that covers the following key areas:

- Introduction to Data Pattern Recognition: Start with an overview of why pattern recognition is crucial in data-driven decision-making. Provide real-world examples of how pattern recognition has impacted your organization or industry.

- Types of Data Patterns: Teach employees to recognize various types of patterns, including trends, seasonality, cycles, and anomalies. Use visual aids and case studies to illustrate each type.

- Data Visualization: Introduce data visualization tools and techniques. Show how different chart types can help reveal patterns effectively. Hands-On exercises with tools like Excel, Tableau, or Python libraries can be highly beneficial.

- Hypothesis Driven Analysis: Teach employees how to formulate hypotheses based on business questions and prior knowledge. Show them how to design experiments or analyses to test these hypotheses.

- Data Interpretation and Communication: Train employees on how to interpret the patterns they discover and communicate these insights clearly and persuasively to technical and non-technical stakeholders.

Step 4: Choose Training Methods

Select appropriate training methods based on your employees' preferences and needs. Consider a mix of the following:

- Gamification Strategy: Select games like Crossy Road or PacMan that have inherent pattern recognition elements. Ensure these games align with your learning objectives.

- Customize or create levels within these games that progressively challenge employees' pattern recognition skills.

- Workshops: Conduct hands-on workshops where employees can practice data pattern recognition using real data sets.

- Online Courses: Provide access to online courses and tutorials on data analysis and visualization.

- Success Sponsorship: Pair less experienced employees with data-savvy mentors for one-on-one guidance.

- Guest Speakers: Invite data analysis or data science experts to give talks or presentations.

- Book Clubs: Encourage employees to read relevant books and discuss their learnings in group settings.

Step 5: Implement Training

Roll out the training program systematically, ensuring it accommodates employees' schedules and workloads. Creating a supportive learning environment that fosters engagement and participation is essential.

Step 6: Hands-On Practice

Encourage employees to apply what they've learned to real work scenarios. Provide them with opportunities to work on projects or analyze data relevant to their roles. This practical experience will reinforce their skills and build confidence.

Step 7: Continuous Feedback and Improvement

Establish a feedback loop where employees can share their experiences and challenges. Use their feedback to adjust the training program and address any issues or concerns.

Step 8: Assess Progress

Periodically reassess employees' skills through quizzes, assignments, or practical exercises to measure their progress and identify areas needing additional attention.

Step 9: Recognition and Rewards

Acknowledge and reward employees who demonstrate significant improvement in data pattern recognition. Recognition can motivate others to actively engage in the learning process.

Step 10: Ongoing Learning

Emphasize the importance of continuous learning in the field of data pattern recognition. Encourage employees to stay updated with the latest tools and techniques, attend conferences, and participate in knowledge-sharing sessions.

Step 11: Evaluate Impact

Measure the training program's impact on the organization's decision-making processes, efficiency, and overall performance. Use key performance indicators (KPIs) to assess how improved data pattern recognition contributes to business success.

By following this structured plan, you can systematically teach and improve employees' skills in recognizing patterns in data, enabling them to make more informed and effective business decisions.

Teaching employees how to understand data and recognize patterns is an investment that can yield substantial returns for your organization. By fostering a culture of data literacy, you empower your team to make better-informed decisions, drive innovation, and stay competitive in a rapidly evolving business landscape.

Remember that data literacy is an ongoing journey; continuous learning and practice are key to success in this field.

Section 10

Cognitive Behavioral Coaching (CBC)

Welcome to the world of Cognitive Behavioral Coaching, where we'll help you unlock the hidden mysteries of your mind, one raised eyebrow at a time.

I know what you're thinking: "Can a coach fix my messy thoughts?" Well, let me assure you, we're not here to rewire your brain like a malfunctioning toaster. Instead, we'll delicately rearrange your mental furniture just enough to convince your brain that it's a well-organized IKEA catalog.

So, grab your coffee, sit back, and get ready to have your irrational fears dismantled faster than you can say, "Why did I ever think I could assemble that bookshelf on my own?"

Chapter 1: Understanding Cognitive Behavioral Coaching

Cognitive Behavioral Coaching is an approach that draws from cognitive behavioral therapy (CBT) principles and applies them to the coaching context. CBT is well-known for its effectiveness in helping individuals recognize and change negative thought patterns and behaviors.

CBC extends these principles to coaching, empowering individuals to identify and address limiting beliefs, attitudes, and behaviors that hinder their performance and well-being.

The Core Principles of CBC

Self-awareness: CBC encourages individuals to become more self-aware of their thoughts, emotions, and behaviors. This self-awareness is the foundation for personal growth and development.

- Identifying limiting beliefs: Coaches work with individuals to identify beliefs and thought patterns that may be holding them back or causing stress and anxiety.

- Behavioral change: CBC helps individuals develop strategies to replace unproductive behaviors with more effective ones.

- Goal setting: Coaches and individuals collaborate to set clear, achievable goals that align with the individual's values and aspirations.

- Accountability: CBC holds individuals accountable for their actions and progress toward their goals.

The Benefits of CBC in the Workplace

- Enhanced Productivity

CBC can significantly contribute to increased productivity in the workplace. By helping employees identify and challenge procrastination, self-doubt, and other productivity-limiting beliefs, coaches enable them to develop effective time management skills and a focus on achieving their goals. Furthermore, CBC equips employees with the tools to manage stress and anxiety, reducing the negative impact of these emotions on productivity.

- Fostering Creativity

Creativity thrives in an environment where individuals are encouraged to explore new ideas and perspectives. CBC promotes creative thinking by helping employees overcome fear of failure and self-criticism. Coaches work with individuals to reframe their thought processes, fostering a more positive and growth-oriented mindset. This shift in thinking allows employees to take risks, experiment with new approaches, and unleash their creative potential.

• Boosting Morale and Job Satisfaction
Employee morale and job satisfaction are closely tied to their sense of personal fulfilment and well-being. CBC contributes to a positive workplace culture by supporting employees in managing stress, building resilience, and developing a more optimistic outlook. When employees feel valued and supported, their morale improves, leading to higher job satisfaction, increased loyalty, and reduced turnover rates.

Chapter 2: Unlocking Change: The Efficacy of Cognitive Behavioral Coaching for Habit Transformation

Cognitive Behavioral Coaching (CBC) can significantly enhance the effectiveness of habit change by addressing both the cognitive (thoughts and beliefs) and behavioral (actions and reactions) aspects of the process.

Here's how CBC can help individuals achieve more successful habit change:

- Self-awareness: CBC starts by helping individuals become more aware of their current habits and the underlying thought patterns that drive them. Through self-reflection and assessment, individuals gain insight into the habits they want to change and the triggers that lead to them.

- Identification of limiting beliefs: CBC encourages individuals to identify any negative or limiting beliefs about their ability to change or the habit itself. These beliefs can be challenged and reframed to promote a more positive and confident mindset.

- Goal setting: CBC assists individuals in setting clear, specific, and achievable goals for habit change. These goals serve as a roadmap for what they want to achieve and provide motivation to stay on track.

- Behavioral strategies: CBC equips individuals with practical strategies to modify their behavior effectively. This includes techniques such as stimulus control (managing environmental cues), self-monitoring (tracking progress), and positive reinforcement (rewarding oneself for progress).

- Cognitive restructuring: In CBC, individuals learn how to identify and replace negative or unhelpful thought patterns with more positive and constructive ones. This helps change the mental narratives associated with the habit and reduce self-sabotage.

- Problem-solving: When individuals encounter obstacles or setbacks in habit change, CBC provides problem-solving skills. Coaches help individuals brainstorm solutions, adapt their strategies, and find ways to overcome challenges.

- Accountability and feedback: Regular check-ins with a coach provide accountability and an opportunity for feedback. These interactions help individuals stay committed to their goals and make necessary adjustments based on their progress.

- Motivation and commitment: CBC explores an individual's values, interests, and reasons for wanting to change a habit. This process strengthens motivation and commitment by aligning habit change with personal goals and values.

- Relapse prevention: CBC teaches individuals strategies to prevent relapses and manage setbacks effectively. Learning to bounce back from slip-ups is crucial for maintaining long-term habit change.

- Skill-building: Sometimes, habit change may require acquiring new skills or knowledge. CBC can guide individuals in developing the necessary skills to support their habit change efforts.

- Sustaining progress: CBC doesn't stop when the new habit is formed; it continues to support individuals in maintaining and integrating the habit into their daily lives.

- Personalization: CBC is highly tailored to the individual's needs, preferences, and circumstances. This personalization enhances the effectiveness of habit change interventions.

By addressing the cognitive and behavioral dimensions of habit change, Cognitive Behavioral Coaching provides a holistic approach that equips individuals with the tools, strategies, and support they need to effectively change their habits.

It recognizes that habit change is not just about willpower but also about understanding and managing the psychological factors that influence behavior. This comprehensive approach can lead to more successful and lasting habit change outcomes.

Practical Cognitive Behavioral Coaching (CBC) Exercises and Tools

Using practical exercises and tools rooted in Cognitive Behavioral Coaching (CBC) holds significant potential for employers seeking to facilitate the development of their employees' cognitive and emotional competencies, elevate their overall performance, and adeptly navigate the complexities of workplace challenges.

In the subsequent discussion, we will explore a selection of these invaluable exercises and tools available for employers to implement.

- Thought Records: Provide employees with thought record templates. They can use these templates to identify and challenge negative or irrational thoughts related to work situations. This helps in changing unhelpful thought patterns.

- Strengths-Based Coaching: Identify and leverage employees' strengths and positive qualities. Use tools like Gallup's StrengthsFinder or VIA Character Strengths to help individuals recognize and utilize their unique strengths.

- Time Management and Prioritization: Teach time management techniques like the Eisenhower Matrix or Pomodoro Technique to help employees become more efficient and productive.

- Behavioral Experiments: Encourage employees to conduct behavioral experiments to test their beliefs and assumptions. For example, if employees believe they're terrible at public speaking, they could experiment by volunteering for a small presentation.

- Goal Setting and Action Planning: Assist employees in setting specific, measurable, achievable, relevant, and time-bound (SMART) goals for their work. Help them create action plans outlining the steps they need to take to achieve these goals.

- ABC Model: Teach employees the ABC model (Antecedent-Behavior-Consequence) to help them understand the relationship between events, reactions, and the consequences. This can address issues related to emotional reactions or problematic behaviors.

- Role-Playing: Use role-playing exercises to help employees practice and improve their interpersonal skills, such as conflict resolution, assertiveness, or giving and receiving feedback.

- Journaling and Self-Reflection: Encourage employees to maintain a journal to record their thoughts, emotions, and experiences at work. Regular self-reflection can help them gain insight into their cognitive patterns.

- Stress Reduction Techniques: Provide training in stress management techniques, such as deep breathing, progressive muscle relaxation, or mindfulness meditation. These tools can help employees cope with workplace stress.

- Cognitive Restructuring Worksheets: Share worksheets or online resources that guide individuals through identifying and challenging negative thought patterns.

- Gratitude Journal: Encourage employees to keep a gratitude journal, where they write down things they're grateful for each day. This practice can promote a positive mindset and reduce negative thinking.

- Positive Affirmations: Encourage employees to create and use positive affirmations to counteract self-doubt and boost confidence.

- Feedback and Self-Assessment Tools: Use performance feedback and self-assessment tools to help employees clearly understand their strengths and areas for improvement.

- Time Management Tools: Offer tools and techniques for effective time management, such as task lists, time blocking, and prioritization strategies.

- Self-Care Plans: Encourage employees to create self-care plans that include activities and practices to promote their physical and emotional well-being.

- Problem-Solving Frameworks: Teach systematic problem-solving approaches, such as the GROW (Goals, Reality, Options, Will) model, to help employees address work-related challenges.

- Visualization and Imagery: Guide employees in using visualization and positive imagery techniques to enhance their performance and build confidence.

- Conflict Resolution Models: Provide resources on conflict resolution models like the Thomas-Kilmann Conflict Mode Instrument to help employees navigate workplace conflicts more effectively.

- Resilience-Building Workshops: Offer workshops or resources focused on building resilience and adapting to change, as resilience is crucial for dealing with workplace stressors.

- Peer Support and Coaching: Encourage peer support and coaching relationships among employees, fostering a culture of mutual assistance and learning.

- Employee Assistance Programs (EAPs): Consider offering EAPs that provide confidential counseling and coaching services to employees facing personal or work-related challenges.

- Online Self-Help Resources: Curate a list of reputable online resources, apps, and websites that employees can access for additional self-help and self-improvement guidance.

When implementing these exercises and tools, creating a supportive and non-judgmental coaching environment is essential, respecting employees' privacy, and providing appropriate training or access to external coaches with expertise in CBC if necessary.

Chapter 3: Cognitive Behavioral Coaching In Action

When applied within organizations, Cognitive Behavioral Coaching (CBC) can be a powerful tool to enhance productivity, and measuring its effectiveness with data and metrics is essential for tracking progress and ensuring a positive impact.

Here's how organizations can use CBC to improve productivity and measure its outcomes:

1. Identify Specific Goals and Objectives:
Define clear, measurable productivity goals for individuals or teams within the organization.
Determine the specific areas where CBC can be most beneficial, such as time management, stress reduction, or leadership skills.

2. Select Key Performance Indicators (KPIs):
Choose KPIs that align with the identified productivity goals. Examples include:

*   Output metrics (e.g., project completion rates, sales targets)
*   Efficiency metrics (e.g., time spent on tasks, error rates)
*   Employee satisfaction and engagement scores
*   Employee turnover rates (attrition)

3. Assess Current Productivity Levels:

- Collect baseline data on the selected KPIs to establish a starting point for measurement.
- Conduct surveys, interviews, or assessments to gather qualitative data on employees' challenges and barriers to productivity.

4. Implement CBC Interventions:

- Provide CBC sessions to individuals or teams to address specific productivity-related issues.
- CBC can help employees identify and challenge unhelpful thought patterns, develop new behaviors, and set realistic goals.

5. Track Progress and Gather Data:

- Continuously monitor and record data on the chosen KPIs throughout the CBC intervention.
- Use quantitative data (e.g., performance metrics) and qualitative data (e.g., employee feedback) to gauge progress.

6. Analyze and Interpret Data:

- Analyze the collected data to identify trends and correlations.
- Look for improvements in the selected KPIs and assess whether they can be attributed to the CBC interventions.

7. Adjust and Refine Coaching Approach:

- Based on the data analysis, adjust the CBC approach as needed.
- Tailor coaching sessions to address emerging issues or

further enhance productivity in specific areas.

8. Measure Return on Investment (ROI):

- Calculate the ROI of CBC interventions by comparing the costs of coaching to the improvements in productivity.
- Consider the long-term impact, such as reduced turnover, improved employee satisfaction, and immediate productivity gains.

9. Provide Feedback and Recognition:

- Share the results of CBC interventions and their impact on productivity with employees and leadership.
- Recognize and reward individuals and teams for their achievements and contributions to productivity improvements.

10. Continuously Improve and Sustain:

- Use the insights gained from data and metrics to refine CBC programs and coaching techniques.
- Continuously support employees in maintaining and building on their productivity gains.

Incorporating data and metrics into the CBC process allows organizations to make informed decisions, demonstrate the effectiveness of coaching programs, and ensure that efforts are aligned with overall productivity and organizational goals.

It also enables a feedback loop for continuous improvement and optimization of coaching strategies.

Section 11

Dangers of
Excess Meeting Culture

Gather 'round, for we are about to embark on a riveting exploration of the truly exhilarating world of excess meeting culture. Yes, you heard it right – meetings, meetings, and more meetings! Because who needs actual work when you can spend your precious time attending meetings that seem to multiply faster than rabbits on a carrot farm?

In this scintillating exposé, we will delve into the myriad dangers of drowning in a sea of meetings, where productivity goes to die, and enthusiasm takes a permanent vacation. But don't worry because we're about to uncover the secrets of how pointless, never-ending meetings can transform your workday into a delightful exercise in futility.

So, grab your favorite notepad (which you probably won't have time to use), put on your most convincing "I care about this meeting" face, and prepare to be astounded by the astounding dangers of the excess meeting culture that has taken the corporate world by storm.

***

In today's fast-paced and dynamic business world, meetings have become integral to organizational culture. They serve as a means of communication, collaboration, and decision-making. However, there's a growing concern that many businesses have fallen into the trap of an excessive meeting culture. While meetings can be valuable, their overabundance can prove counterproductive in numerous ways. In this chapter, we will explore why having an excessive meeting culture in business can hinder productivity, creativity, and overall success.

The Myth of Productivity

Meetings are often seen as a tool to boost productivity, but they can have the opposite effect. Consider the time spent preparing for a meeting, attending it, and recovering from it. This time investment often exceeds the actual productive work done in the meeting. A study by Doodle, a scheduling software company, found that the average professional spends nearly 30 hours a month in unproductive meetings. This time could be better utilized for strategic planning, focused work, or skill development.

Chapter 1: The Law of Diminishing Returns in Meetings

The law of diminishing returns, a fundamental concept in economics, asserts that as you increase the use of a particular input while keeping other inputs constant, the incremental output gained from that input will eventually decrease. In the context of excessive meetings, this principle applies quite aptly.

When an organization conducts meetings judiciously, it can yield substantial benefits. These benefits might include increased clarity on project objectives, alignment of team members, and informed decision-making. However, as meetings become more frequent and routine, their value begins to decline, and several key factors contribute to this decline:

Reduced Engagement

When meetings occur too frequently, participants often find themselves in a state of meeting fatigue. The novelty and anticipation of a productive discussion wear off, leading to decreased engagement. Attendees may start viewing meetings as obligatory rather than opportunities for meaningful collaboration. As a result, their active participation dwindles, and they may mentally check out or multitask during the meeting, further reducing its effectiveness.

Time Fragmentation

Frequent meetings disrupt an individual's workflow and concentration. It's akin to repeatedly interrupting a manufacturing process to recalibrate the machinery – each interruption consumes time and mental resources.

As participants are pulled away from their core tasks, their productivity suffers. This time fragmentation can lead to a lack of continuity in their work, making it harder to maintain focus and complete tasks efficiently.

Information Overload

In a culture of excess meetings, participants may become inundated with information that may not immediately be relevant to their roles or responsibilities. This information overload can lead to confusion and overwhelm, making it difficult for individuals to process and prioritize the details discussed in meetings.
Consequently, they may struggle to retain and apply important insights, diminishing the return on their investment of time and attention.

Erosion of Accountability

With too many meetings, individuals may perceive themselves as mere attendees, not responsible decision-makers. They might believe their input is less impactful and that the final decisions will be made elsewhere or during another meeting. This erosion of accountability can lead to a lack of ownership and commitment among team members, reducing the likelihood of actionable outcomes.

Impact on Creativity

When used judiciously, meetings can be a forum for brainstorming and creative problem-solving. However, frequent and routine meetings tend to become more procedural and focused on updates and status reports. This shift away from creative thinking can hinder innovation and the generation of fresh ideas, which are often essential for business growth and adaptation to changing circumstances.

Striking a Balance

Organizations must strike a balance between collaboration and individual productivity to mitigate the adverse effects of diminishing returns in meetings. This balance can be achieved through a combination of strategies, including:

- Meeting Purpose: Ensure that each meeting has a clearly defined purpose and that attendees understand how their contributions are vital to achieving its objectives.

- Agenda and Time Management: Develop a concise agenda and adhere to time limits. Avoid delving into tangential discussions that prolong meetings unnecessarily.

- Alternatives to Meetings: Consider alternative communication methods, such as emails, project management tools, or asynchronous discussions, for routine updates or non-urgent matters.

- Feedback and Adaptation: Encourage open feedback from meeting participants to continuously improve the effectiveness of meetings. Adapt and refine your meeting processes based on this feedback.

- Critical Evaluation: Regularly assess the necessity of recurring meetings. If a meeting consistently fails to deliver value, consider discontinuing it or replacing it with a more efficient format.

Just as the law of diminishing returns predicts, the value of meetings diminishes as their frequency increases. Excessive meetings lead to reduced engagement, time fragmentation, information overload, and a decline in creativity.

Organizations that recognize these dynamics and implement strategies to maintain the quality and purpose of their meetings will find themselves better positioned to achieve their goals while preserving the time and energy of their team members.

Creativity and Innovation Suffer

Excessive meetings can stifle creativity and innovation within a company. Creativity often flourishes in environments where individuals have time to think, experiment, and explore new ideas. Employees who are constantly tied up in meetings may not have the mental space or time to innovate and think outside the box.

Moreover, meetings can unintentionally create an environment where conformity is rewarded over creative dissent.

Decision-Making Paralysis

Meetings are often called to make decisions, but having too many of them can lead to decision-making paralysis. When decisions are deferred to meetings, the organization's decision-making process becomes slower, and individuals may become hesitant to decide independently. This can lead to missed opportunities and a lack of agility in responding to changing market conditions.

Erosion of Employee Morale

An excessive meeting culture can also erode employee morale. When employees feel that their time is wasted in meetings that don't contribute to their work or the company's success, they become disengaged and unmotivated. This can result in decreased job satisfaction and higher turnover rates as employees seek workplaces that value their time and contributions.

Costly Endeavors

Meetings come with a cost – not just in terms of time, but also financially. Consider the salaries of everyone attending a meeting, the cost of meeting space, and any materials or resources used during the meeting.

These expenses can increase quickly, especially in large organizations with frequent meetings. It's crucial for businesses to weigh the cost against the benefits of each meeting and consider alternative ways to achieve their objectives more efficiently.

✸ Chapter 2: Strategic Drift

Strategic drift is a concept that often arises in organizations characterized by an excessive meeting culture. It describes a gradual and unintentional deviation from an organization's originally defined strategic goals and long-term vision.

This drift occurs when the organization becomes too preoccupied with addressing immediate concerns and short-term challenges, ultimately losing sight of its core mission and values.

Here's a closer look at strategic drift and its consequences:

Causes of Strategic Drift

- Overemphasis on Tactical Concerns: In an environment where meetings constantly revolve around troubleshooting and firefighting, the organization may become hyper-focused on immediate issues at the expense of long-term planning. This overemphasis on tactical concerns can lead to a neglect of strategic initiatives.

- Short-Term Metrics: Organizations driven by an excess meeting culture might prioritize short-term metrics and outcomes, such as meeting targets for the current quarter, over longer-term strategic objectives. This narrow focus can disconnect day-to-day operations and the broader strategic plan.

- Reactive decision-making: Frequent meetings can promote a reactive decision-making culture. Instead of proactively shaping their future, organizations react to external pressures and crises, leading to knee-jerk decisions that don't align with the original strategic vision.

Consequences of Strategic Drift

- Loss of Competitive Advantage: When an organization strays from its strategic path, it may lose its competitive edge. Competitors focused on long-term objectives can outmaneuver the drifting organization, eroding its market position.

- Confusion and Disorientation: Employees and stakeholders may become confused about the organization's direction when it experiences strategic drift. This lack of clarity can lead to reduced morale, increased turnover, and a weakened sense of purpose among team members.

- Resource Misallocation: Resources, including time, budget, and talent, maybe misallocated toward initiatives that do not align with the organization's strategic goals. This inefficiency can hinder progress and undermine the organization's ability to achieve its long-term vision.

- Ineffective Leadership: Leaders may struggle to inspire and guide their teams when the organization experiences strategic drift. Without a clear strategic direction, leadership can become uncertain and less effective in setting priorities and motivating employees.

Addressing Strategic Drift

- Strategic Review: Regularly assess the organization's strategic goals and ensure they remain relevant in the evolving business landscape. This involves revisiting the mission, vision, and values and making necessary adjustments.

- Strategic Communication: Communicate the organization's long-term vision and strategic goals to all stakeholders. Ensure employees understand their roles in achieving these objectives, fostering alignment and commitment.

- Balanced Meeting Culture: Streamline and optimize the meeting culture within the organization to strike a balance between addressing immediate concerns and focusing on long-term strategy. Implement meeting policies that prioritize strategic discussions.

- Data-driven decision-making: Encourage data-driven decision-making to ensure that strategic choices are based on evidence and analysis rather than reactions to short-term challenges.

- Leadership Commitment: Leaders must champion the organization's strategic goals and exemplify a commitment to long-term vision. Their actions and decisions should consistently reinforce the importance of strategic alignment.

Strategic drift is a pervasive challenge that can emerge in organizations with an excessive meeting culture. To combat it, organizations must prioritize long-term strategic planning, maintain open lines of communication, and foster a culture of strategic focus.

By taking these steps, organizations can avoid the drift and remain on course to achieve their core mission and values.

⊛ Chapter 3: The Path to a More Effective Meeting Culture

Organizations must adopt a more mindful approach to scheduling and conducting meetings to combat the counterproductive effects of an excessive meeting culture. This includes:

• Assess the Current Meeting Culture:
Start by evaluating your organization's current meeting culture. Gather feedback from employees, leaders, and stakeholders to identify pain points and areas for improvement.

• Define Clear Meeting Objectives:
Ensure that every meeting has a specific and well-defined purpose. Meetings should serve to make decisions, share information, brainstorm ideas, or solve problems.

• Implement Meeting Guidelines:
Establish clear guidelines for meetings. This includes setting agendas, assigning roles (e.g., facilitator, timekeeper), and determining expected outcomes.

• Reduce Meeting Frequency:
Evaluate whether all scheduled meetings are necessary. Eliminate or combine meetings that do not contribute to the organization's goals.

• Embrace Technology:
Utilize technology for virtual meetings, collaboration, and document sharing. Ensure that the necessary tools and resources are readily available and user-friendly.

• Set Time Limits:
Implement time limits for meetings. Encourage participants to stick to the agenda and stay on track to prevent meetings from running over their allotted time.

- Foster Inclusivity:

Create an inclusive meeting environment where all voices are heard. Encourage diverse perspectives and ensure that quieter team members have an opportunity to speak.

- Provide Training:

Offer training on effective meeting management and communication skills for leaders and participants. This can include time management, active listening, and conflict resolution.

- Use Productivity Tools:

Implement productivity tools and software to streamline meetings. Project management software, calendar apps, and note-taking apps can enhance organization and follow-up.

- Promote Accountability:

Hold participants accountable for meeting outcomes and action items. Follow up on commitments made during meetings and track progress.

- Experiment with Meeting Formats:

Try different meeting formats, such as standup meetings, walking meetings, or asynchronous communication, to keep things fresh and engaging.

- Monitor and Adjust:

Continuously assess the effectiveness of your new meeting culture. Gather feedback, track key performance indicators, and be open to making adjustments as needed.

- Lead by Example:

Leadership plays a critical role in shaping meeting culture. Leaders should model good meeting practices, demonstrate punctuality, and reinforce the importance of effective meetings.

- Celebrate Successes:
Recognize and celebrate successful meetings that achieve their objectives efficiently. Positive reinforcement can encourage continued improvement.

- Communicate the Changes:
Communicate the changes in meeting culture to the entire organization. Explain the rationale behind the changes and provide resources for employees to adapt.

- Solicit Feedback Regularly:
Create a feedback loop for ongoing improvement. Encourage team members to share their thoughts on meeting culture and use this feedback to make necessary adjustments.

- Document and Share Best Practices:
Compile a repository of best practices for effective meetings within your organization and share these with all employees.

- Evaluate the Impact:
Periodically assess the impact of your efforts on meeting culture, productivity, and employee satisfaction. Use this data to refine your approach.

- Review and Adapt:
Stay flexible and open to evolving your meeting culture as the organization's needs change.

Establishing a more effective meeting culture demands an unwavering commitment from all organizational stakeholders. It is not merely a one-time initiative but rather a long-term, ongoing commitment to efficient and meaningful communication principles. It requires a collective acknowledgment of the importance of meetings as integral to the organization's success and a pledge to allocate time and resources accordingly.

Continuous improvement is the cornerstone of this endeavor. Organizations must adopt a mindset of perpetual refinement, encouraging team members to actively seek opportunities to optimize their meeting processes.

Regular feedback mechanisms, such as post-meeting evaluations, can provide valuable insights into what works well and needs improvement. Embracing technological advancements and best practices in meeting facilitation can also contribute to the overall enhancement of the meeting culture.

Adaptability is essential in maintaining an effective meeting culture. The business landscape is dynamic, and external factors, such as market conditions or technological innovations, can necessitate shifts in meeting practices. An adaptable culture allows organizations to respond swiftly and effectively to these changes, ensuring that meetings remain aligned with organizational goals.

Following this comprehensive approach, your organization can systematically cultivate a meeting culture prioritizing productivity by ensuring that meetings have clear objectives and desired outcomes. It underscores the importance of purposefulness, emphasizing that meetings should only be convened when necessary, with a well-defined agenda that serves a specific purpose.

Finally, it underscores the critical need for efficiency, advocating for the efficient allocation of time, resources, and participant contributions during meetings.
Creating an effective meeting culture is not an isolated event but an ongoing journey that requires dedication, continuous refinement, and adaptability. By embracing these principles and committing to this action plan, your organization can foster a culture that values and consistently achieves productive, purposeful, and efficient meetings, ultimately contributing to enhanced organizational success.

Section 12

Using New Technology and Tools

Oh, the joy of embracing new collaborative tools in the workplace! Because, you know, who doesn't love the thrill of adapting to new technology in the middle of an already chaotic workday? It's almost as delightful as watching paint dry. But, believe it or not, there's a silver lining here.

As much as they might make us roll our eyes, these tools have their perks.

First, they're a true employee satisfaction booster. Who wouldn't be over the moon about learning a new system that might or might not improve their workflow? It's like a puzzle you didn't ask for, but it keeps you on your toes!

Plus, employees adore the extra time it takes to figure out how to use these tools effectively. It's like a mini-vacation from their actual job.

As for retention, let's say that the chance to struggle with a new tool and potentially fail miserably at it is an excellent way to keep employees on their toes. After all, who wants to risk leaving a job they've invested years in just because they can't decipher the latest software update? It's job security at its finest!

And productivity? Oh boy, these new tools are a marvel. They might slow you down at first, but you'll be lightning-fast once you've spent hours, days, or weeks mastering them. Think of it as the long and winding road to productivity paradise. It might take a while, but the destination is worth it. And all those countless hours spent troubleshooting? Well, they're character-building.

In all seriousness, while embracing new collaborative tools can be a bit of a hassle initially, they do have the potential to enhance employee satisfaction, retention, and productivity.

Once everyone gets the hang of them, these tools can streamline processes, improve communication, and make work more efficient. So, as much as we joke about the challenges, they are, in the end, a step toward a more productive and connected workplace.

***

In today's rapidly changing business world, staying ahead of the curve has never been more crucial. The workplace of the 21st century is a dynamic ecosystem, continually shaped by technological advancements and shifting paradigms. Now more than ever, organizations must adapt to these changes to survive and thrive in an increasingly competitive world.

Central to this transformation is adopting new productivity and communication tools, and redefining how work is done. These tools, often driven by digital innovation, are more than passing trends; they are becoming the cornerstones of modern workplace efficiency and collaboration. From project management platforms that streamline workflows to real-time messaging apps that connect teams across continents, these tools promise to revolutionize how we work, communicate, and ultimately succeed.

However, embracing change can be daunting. The familiar routines and processes that have guided us for years (email) can feel like comfortable old friends, even if they no longer serve us as well as they once did. Yet, as with any significant shift, boundless opportunities arise when we open our arms to new possibilities.

In this exploration of embracing new productivity and communication tools in the workplace, we embark on a journey of transformation. Together, we will uncover why these tools are not mere novelties but essential catalysts for growth. We will delve into the challenges and reservations accompanying this change and offer strategies to overcome them.

Most importantly, we will discover how these tools can empower individuals, teams, and organizations to reach new heights of productivity, efficiency, and innovation.
Whether you are a seasoned business leader looking to lead your organization into the future or an individual contributor seeking to enhance your productivity, this guide will equip you with the knowledge, strategies, and inspiration needed to embrace new productivity and communication tools confidently and enthusiastically.

Chapter 1: It All Begins With Communication

Clear communication with employees is essential for organizations for several compelling reasons:

- Alignment with Goals: When employees have a clear understanding of the organization's mission, vision, values, and strategic goals, they are more likely to work toward those objectives. Clear communication helps align individual and team efforts with the organization's broader goals, fostering a sense of purpose and direction.

- Increased Engagement: Engaged employees are more committed, motivated, and productive. Clear communication keeps employees informed about company updates, changes, and opportunities. It also provides a platform for them to voice their concerns and ideas, which fosters a sense of involvement and engagement.

- Improved Decision-Making: Effective communication ensures employees access the information they need to make informed decisions. This can lead to better problem-solving, innovation, and more efficient organizational decision-making processes.

- Reduced Confusion and Misunderstandings: Clear communication helps prevent misunderstandings, conflicts, and confusion. When expectations, roles, and responsibilities are communicated, employees are less likely to make mistakes or duplicate efforts, leading to smoother operations.

- Enhanced Productivity: Employees can work more efficiently when they know what is expected of them and have access to the necessary resources and information. Clear communication reduces time wasted searching for information or clarifying tasks, ultimately boosting productivity.

- Change Management: Organizations often change, whether through restructuring, new policies, or technological advancements. Clear communication is crucial to help employees understand the reasons for change, how it will impact them, and what is expected of them during the transition.

- Employee Satisfaction and Retention: Employees who feel heard and well-informed are more likely to be satisfied with their jobs and stay with the organization. High turnover rates can be costly, so clear communication can help retain valuable talent.

- Safety and Compliance: Clear communication is critical for security and compliance in specific industries, such as healthcare or manufacturing. Employees must understand safety protocols, regulatory requirements, and emergency procedures to protect themselves and others.

- Innovation and Idea Sharing: Clear communication encourages employees to share their ideas, feedback, and suggestions. This can lead to innovation, process improvements, and identifying new organizational opportunities.

- Brand Reputation: External communication often relies on internal communication. Employees who understand and believe in the organization's values and mission are more likely to represent the company positively to customers, partners, and the public, enhancing the organization's brand reputation.

- Legal and Ethical Considerations: Failure to communicate important information to employees, primarily legal and ethical matters, can lead to legal liabilities and damage the organization's reputation. Clear communication helps mitigate these risks.

Clear communication with employees is not just a good practice but a fundamental necessity for organizations. It promotes alignment, engagement, productivity, and safety while reducing confusion and fostering a positive work environment. Organizations that prioritize clear communication are better equipped to adapt to change, make informed decisions, and achieve their goals.

Tools like Microsoft Teams, Google Workplace, Slack, and similar collaborative platforms have revolutionized how companies communicate, fostering faster and more creative interactions than traditional email-based communication.

These platforms offer real-time messaging, file sharing, video conferencing, and integrations with other productivity apps, enabling teams to collaborate seamlessly. Unlike emails, which often result in lengthy back-and-forth exchanges, these tools facilitate instant messaging, allowing employees to seek clarification, share ideas, and make decisions swiftly. Features like threaded conversations, customizable channels, and notification settings further streamline communication, reducing clutter and increasing focus.

Additionally, integrating third-party apps and bots enhances creativity by automating repetitive tasks, promoting innovative problem-solving, and fostering a more dynamic and interconnected work environment. These tools expedite communication and empower teams to think and collaborate more creatively, ultimately driving productivity and innovation.

Chapter 2:
After Clear Communication - Productivity, Collaboration and Camaraderie Arrives

Effective project management begins with clearly communicating goals and objectives before work commences. This initial step sets the foundation for a successful project by aligning team members and stakeholders with a shared vision. It fosters a sense of purpose and commitment when everyone understands what needs to be achieved and why.

However, it doesn't stop there. Utilizing specialized applications to track progress and maintain highly visible communication channels throughout the project's lifecycle is equally crucial. These tools enable teams to stay on track and facilitate real-time collaboration, making it easier to address challenges, adapt to changes, and maintain accountability.

By combining clear communication of objectives with robust project management software, organizations can significantly enhance their ability to complete tasks efficiently, expedite project timelines, and ultimately achieve better outcomes.

In today's fast-paced digital age, the success of businesses and teams often hinges on their ability to harness the power of collaboration and innovation. Thankfully, many productivity tools and platforms have emerged to facilitate these processes. When used correctly and practically, tools like Slack, Google Workspace, and many others can significantly accelerate productivity, ideation, and collaboration and even inject fun into the work environment.

Let's explore some examples of how these tools can make a difference:

Slack

- Real-Time Communication: Slack enables instant messaging, allowing team members to communicate swiftly, and eliminating email delays. For instance, when a team works on a project with tight deadlines, they can quickly share updates, ask questions, and receive prompt feedback.

- Channels for Focus: Slack's channel feature organizes conversations into specific topics or projects. This helps teams stay organized, preventing cluttered inboxes and streamlining discussions. For instance, a marketing team might have channels dedicated to social media, email campaigns, and content creation.

- Integration with Other Tools: Slack integrates seamlessly with various productivity and project management tools, such as Trello, Asana, and Google Drive. This means that files, tasks, and notifications can be centralized in one place, simplifying collaboration and boosting efficiency.

Google Workspace

- Real-Time Collaboration on Documents: Google Workspace, including Google Docs, Sheets, and Slides, allows multiple users to edit documents simultaneously. This real-time collaboration can significantly speed up the ideation and content creation process. For instance, a team of writers can brainstorm and draft articles in a single document.

- Shared Calendars: Google Calendar within Workspace enables teams to schedule meetings and appointments efficiently. By sharing calendars, couples can avoid scheduling conflicts and coordinate meetings faster. This is especially useful for teams working across different time zones.

- Collaborative Emailing: With Google Workspace, multiple team members can access and collaborate on emails in shared inboxes. This is particularly valuable for customer support teams, as they can work together to resolve inquiries more effectively.

Zoom

- Virtual Meetings: Zoom has become synonymous with virtual meetings and webinars. It allows teams to hold face-to-face meetings, screen-sharing sessions, and webinars regardless of geographical boundaries. This accelerates decision-making, brainstorming, and creativity.

- Recording Meetings: Zoom enables users to record meetings and webinars. This helps archive meaningful discussions, training sessions, and presentations, ensuring that valuable information isn't lost and can be revisited anytime.

- Breakout Rooms: Zoom's breakout room feature allows larger meetings to be split into smaller, focused groups. This promotes collaboration, as participants can ideate in smaller, more intimate settings before regrouping to share their findings.

Slack bots and Chatbots

- Automation: Slackbots and chatbots can automate repetitive tasks, such as data retrieval, file sharing, and reminders. For example, a Slackbot can provide team members with quick access to frequently used documents, reducing the time spent searching for information.

- Enhancing Fun: Some chatbots are designed to inject humor and fun into the work environment. They can share jokes, trivia and engage in light-hearted conversations, promoting a positive team culture and reducing stress.

These tools and platforms have revolutionized the way teams work together, fostering greater productivity, ideation, collaboration, and even injecting elements of fun into the workplace.

When used strategically and aligned with team objectives, they can lead to faster cycles of innovation and achievement, making the modern workplace a more efficient and enjoyable space for everyone involved.

Workplace-shared tools and their in-app functions have undergone a remarkable transformation in recent years, adapting to the ever-evolving needs of modern professionals. What's particularly fascinating is how these tools are increasingly being utilized in new and exciting ways, often extending beyond their original purposes. This trend is driven by technological advancements, creative user innovation, and the growing demand for more versatile and collaborative work environments.

One prominent example of this phenomenon is the ubiquitous use of communication and collaboration platforms. While these tools were initially designed for text messaging, video conferencing, and file sharing, they now serve as multifunctional hubs for work-related activities.

Teams are finding innovative ways to integrate project management, customer relationship management (CRM), and even automation functions within these platforms. This not only streamlines workflows but also encourages more seamless cross-functional collaboration.

Moreover, shared tools are increasingly being leveraged to facilitate employee well-being and engagement. Features like in-app surveys and sentiment analysis are being used to gauge employee satisfaction and identify areas for improvement. Some organizations have even gamified their internal communication tools, turning mundane tasks into interactive challenges that boost morale and productivity.

Beyond the workplace, these tools are transcending their professional boundaries. For instance, augmented reality (AR) and virtual reality (VR) elements are being incorporated into shared tools for immersive training experiences.

Similarly, data analytics tools are enabling users to extract insights from their personal lives, from tracking fitness goals to managing household finances. This expansion of functionality beyond the workplace demonstrates the versatility and adaptability of these tools, making them indispensable in the digital age.

Workplace-shared tools and their in-app functions continually evolve, offering exciting opportunities for innovation and collaboration. As technology continues to advance and user needs evolve, we can expect to see these tools serving as even more versatile, multifunctional platforms that extend their utility far beyond their original design, enhancing productivity and connectivity in both professional and personal spheres.

Chapter 3: From Inbox Zero to Inbox Hero

Ah, the glorious invention of email, a timeless masterpiece of modern communication. Legend has it that email was invented by a tech-savvy caveman who got tired of carving stone tablets and decided to send a digital message to his fellow cave-dwelling comrades using his trusty pet pterodactyl as a carrier pigeon. Okay, maybe not exactly like that, but email feels ancient in today's tech-savvy world.

Why, you ask, does email continue to be used so diligently when we have an abundance of shiny new productivity and collaboration tools at our fingertips, like Teams, Google Workspaces, Slack, and more? Well, it's quite simple, really. Email has been around since the dinosaurs roamed the Earth, or at least since the 1970s, which, in tech terms, might as well be prehistoric.

First of all, there's the nostalgia factor. Who doesn't love receiving a cluttered inbox full of chain letters, spam, and those oh-so-important "reply all" messages? It's like a digital treasure hunt where the real prize is buried beneath an avalanche of promotional offers and cat videos. And let's not forget the thrill of hitting "send" on an email and then immediately regretting it, desperately searching for the elusive "recall" button. It's like playing Russian roulette with your professional reputation!

But in all seriousness, email, with all its quirks and limitations, continues to endure because it's a familiar and universal tool. It's the low-tech duct-tape solution that everyone can use, regardless of their tech-savviness so while we may have fancier tools in our tech toolbox, email soldiers on, like that trusty old typewriter collecting dust in your attic, reminding us that sometimes the classics never go out of style.

And let's not forget the charming email chains that resemble a never-ending relay race, where each recipient adds their two cents before passing the digital baton. It's like a slow-motion conversation that spans days, with participants from different time zones chiming in at their leisure. Who needs real-time collaboration when you can savor the suspense of waiting for that one colleague who always replies with "Thanks!" just to keep the chain alive? Truly, email is the social glue that binds our digital lives together, one "Reply" at a time.

While modern collaboration tools may offer slick interfaces and the promise of seamless teamwork, email remains a quirky, enduring relic of the digital age. It's the constant in an ever-evolving tech landscape, reminding us that sometimes, simplicity and tradition have their place—even if that place is buried beneath thousands of unread messages.

So, embrace the chaos of your inbox and remember that email isn't just a communication tool; it's an adventure waiting to unfold in the form of unopened attachments and cryptic subject lines.

Modernizing Workplace Communication and Productivity

In today's fast-paced business environment, organizations must adapt to modern workplace trends and technologies to remain competitive. One critical area to address is communication and productivity.

Relying solely on email for communication can hinder efficiency and employee morale. This guide will outline steps for organizations to pivot away from sole reliance on email and embrace more modern workplace applications and tools to improve communication, productivity, and morale.

Step 1: Assess Your Current Email Usage

Before making any changes, it's essential to understand how email is currently used within your organization. Conduct surveys, interviews, or analytics reviews to determine:
1. The volume of emails sent and received.
2. Common communication challenges or bottlenecks.
3. Employee preferences and pain points related to email.

Step 2: Identify Modern Communication Tools

Explore and identify modern communication tools and applications that can complement or replace email. Consider options such as:

1. Team Messaging Apps: Platforms like Slack, Microsoft Teams, or Discord enable real-time messaging, file sharing, and integration with other tools.

2. Collaboration Suites: Google Workspace or Microsoft 365 offers a range of collaboration tools, including shared documents, calendars, and video conferencing.
3. Project Management Software: Tools like Trello, Asana, or Monday.com help teams organize tasks and projects efficiently.

4. Intranet and Knowledge Bases: Implementing an internal website or knowledge base can centralize information and reduce the need for email inquiries.

Step 3: Set Clear Objectives

Define clear objectives for transitioning away from email, such as:

1. Reducing Email Overload: Aim to decrease the number of non-essential emails and interruptions.

2. Streamlining Communication: Enhance communication by using real-time messaging and collaboration tools for quick responses.

3. Improving Productivity: Implement tools and practices that boost productivity, like task management and shared calendars.

4. Boosting Morale: Create a more connected and engaged workforce by facilitating easy communication and reducing stress related to email overload.

Step 4: Provide Training and Support

To effectively provide training and support for new workplace tools, a structured and comprehensive approach is essential to ensure that employees not only adopt these tools but also feel comfortable using them.

Firstly, a well-thought-out training program should be developed. This program should encompass various learning modalities, such as in-person workshops, webinars, written guides, and video tutorials, to cater to diverse learning preferences. The training should begin with an introduction to the tool's purpose and benefits, followed by step-by-step instructions on how to use it. Hands-on practice sessions and real-world scenarios can be integrated to reinforce learning.

Furthermore, it's crucial to establish clear channels of communication for ongoing support. Create a dedicated helpdesk or support team that employees can reach out to with questions or issues related to the new tools. Regularly scheduled "office hours" or drop-in sessions can provide opportunities for one-on-one or group assistance, fostering a sense of personalized support.

Additionally, feedback mechanisms should be put in place to gather input from employees about their experiences with the tools. This feedback can help identify pain points and areas for improvement, leading to continuous refinement of training materials and tools themselves. Encourage a culture of peer support where more experienced users can mentor and assist their colleagues, creating a collaborative environment that eases the learning curve.

Monitoring and tracking employee progress is another essential aspect. Utilize analytics to gauge adoption rates and identify any areas where additional training or support may be required. Recognize and reward early adopters to motivate others.

Providing training and support for new workplace tools is not a one-time event but an ongoing process that requires planning, communication, feedback, and adaptation. By implementing these strategies, employees are more likely to embrace new tools with confidence, enhancing their productivity and contributing to the organization's overall success.

Step 5: Develop Communication Guidelines

Create clear guidelines on how to use the new communication tools effectively. Cover topics like:

1. Etiquette: Encourage respectful and professional communication.

2. File Organization: Promote organized file sharing and naming conventions.

3. Response Times: Set expectations for response times on different platforms.

4. Security: Educate employees on data security and privacy practices.

Step 6: Monitor and Adjust

Continuously monitor the adoption of new tools and gather feedback from employees. Use analytics to assess the impact on communication and productivity. Be prepared to make adjustments and improvements based on feedback and evolving needs.

Step 7: Foster a Culture of Collaboration

Encourage a culture of collaboration and open communication within your organization. Recognize and reward employees who actively engage with the new tools and contribute to a more efficient and connected workplace.

Transitioning away from sole reliance on email to modern workplace applications and tools is a strategic move that can significantly improve communication, productivity, and morale within your organization. By following these steps and embracing the latest technology trends, you can create a more dynamic, efficient, and engaged work environment.

Chapter 4: Listening in a Modern World

Quality assurance plays a pivotal role in ensuring the delivery of an outstanding Customer Experience (CX). In the contemporary and swiftly evolving digital realm, the traditional approach of relying solely on manual quality checks is fraught with challenges.

Not only do manual checks consume valuable time, but they also remain susceptible to the inherent fallibility of human judgment, potentially leading to oversight and inconsistencies. This comprehensive guide aims to shed light on the myriad advantages inherent in the adoption of automated quality assurance tools within the realm of CX.

Furthermore, it offers a meticulously crafted, step-by-step roadmap designed to facilitate the seamless integration and efficient operationalization of these cutting-edge tools within your CX framework. By harnessing the power of automation, organizations can not only expedite their quality assessment processes but also elevate the overall CX to unprecedented levels of excellence.

Benefits of Automated Quality Assurance in CX

- Consistency: Automated tools ensure that the same set of criteria and standards are applied consistently across all interactions, reducing variability in customer experiences.

- Efficiency: Manual quality checks can be labor-intensive and slow. Automation speeds up the process, allowing teams to focus on more strategic tasks.

- Accuracy: Automation eliminates human errors, leading to more accurate evaluations and higher-quality feedback.

- Scalability: As your business grows, automated tools can adapt and scale to handle increased volumes of customer interactions without a proportional increase in resources.

- Data-Driven Insights: Automated tools generate data and analytics, providing valuable insights into CX trends and areas for improvement.

Launching and Operationalizing Automated Quality Assurance Tools

Step 1: Define Your Quality Standards

- Identify Key Metrics: Determine the CX metrics that matter most to your business, such as response time, resolution rate, or sentiment analysis.

- Establish Benchmarks: Define performance benchmarks based on historical data or industry standards.

- Create Evaluation Criteria: Develop clear criteria and guidelines for evaluating interactions, including call scripts, email templates, or messaging/chat responses.

Step 2: Select the Right Tools

- Research and Evaluate Tools: Explore automated quality assurance tools on the market. Consider factors like compatibility with your existing systems, scalability, and user-friendliness.

- Demo and Pilot: Request demos and conduct pilot programs to assess how well the tool aligns with your quality standards and processes.

Step 3: Integrate with CX Channels

- Integration Planning: Work closely with your IT department to integrate the selected tool with your CX channels, such as phone systems, chat platforms, and email.

- Data Mapping: Ensure data flows seamlessly between your CX systems and the quality assurance tool for evaluation and reporting.

Step 4: Train Your Team

- User Training: Train your CX team members on how to use the automated tool effectively. Provide hands-on training sessions and reference materials.

- Feedback Loop: Establish a feedback loop where team members can provide input on tool usability and effectiveness.

Step 5: Set Up Automation Rules

- Configuration: Configure the tool to apply your predefined evaluation criteria and benchmarks automatically.

- Customization: Tailor the tool to your specific needs, such as language preferences, sentiment analysis, or specific evaluation forms.

Step 6: Monitor and Analyze

- Real-time Monitoring: Continuously monitor interactions in real-time to identify issues promptly.

- Data Analytics: Leverage the data and analytics generated by the tool to identify trends and areas for improvement.

Step 7: Iterate and Improve

- Feedback Loops: Encourage ongoing feedback from your CX team and customers to refine your quality standards and tool configuration.

- Continuous Improvement: Use the insights from the tool to make data-driven improvements to your CX processes.

Automated quality assurance tools are invaluable for enhancing CX by ensuring consistency, efficiency, accuracy, scalability, and data-driven insights. By following these steps to launch and operationalize such tools, your organization can provide exceptional customer experiences and stay competitive in today's market.

Summary

New tools and applications for workplace communication, project management, and collaboration seem to emerge almost daily. These technological advancements have undoubtedly revolutionized the way teams operate, making it easier than ever to connect, collaborate, and manage projects. However, amidst this technological revolution, it is crucial for leaders to remember that the fundamental principles of strong, transparent communication and objective goal measurement remain as vital as ever.

While new tools can enhance efficiency and streamline processes, they are only as effective as the people using them. Leaders must recognize that technology alone cannot foster effective teamwork and project success. The foundation of any successful endeavor still lies in clear, transparent communication. No matter how advanced the communication tools become, leaders should emphasize the importance of open and honest dialogue within their teams.

Encouraging team members to share ideas, concerns, and feedback ensures that everyone is on the same page and aligned with the project's goals.

Furthermore, the proliferation of technology does not negate the need for objective goal measurement. In fact, it accentuates its importance. With access to an abundance of data and analytics, leaders have more tools at their disposal than ever before to track progress and measure outcomes. By setting clear, measurable objectives and regularly assessing progress against these benchmarks, leaders can ensure that their teams remain focused on achieving tangible results.

While new tools and applications for workplace communication and project management continue to emerge, they should be seen as enablers rather than replacements for essential leadership practices. Leaders must prioritize strong, transparent communication and objective goal measurement to guide their teams toward success in an increasingly digital world. By combining the power of technology with these timeless principles, organizations can foster a culture of productivity, collaboration, and innovation.

SDSS Summary

In this age of constant technological advancements, where new tools and apps for workplace communication and project management pop up faster than mushrooms after a rain, someone has finally had the epiphany that good old-fashioned communication and setting clear goals are still important. Who would have thought?

While we're all dazzled by the shiny new gadgets and software that promise to make our work lives more accessible, it turns out that they're not a magic potion for success. Do you mean to tell me that even with all these fancy tools, we still need to talk to each other? Astonishing.

Not only do we need to communicate, but we should also measure our goals objectively. What a novel concept! I mean, who needs data and analytics to track progress when you can just rely on hope and chance, right?

Let's not forget the basics in this brave new world of technological wonder. Communication? Yep, it's still essential. Setting clear goals? That hasn't gone out of style either. Who would have guessed that the foundations of good teamwork and project success are still rooted in these ancient principles?

Bravo, modern leaders, for reminding us of these timeless truths amidst the chaos of the digital revolution.

About the Authors

Tim Keefe is the founder and CEO of Transform-CX. He believes in providing clients with customer and employee service solutions leveraging people, process, and technology.

Tim has decades of industry experience in customer service, technology, operations, customer management and business consulting.

As a very hands-on consultant, Tim has seen firsthand how companies and organizations struggled with antiquated and often expensive processes that don't work.

SDSS was born out of Tim's experience and frustration. A lot of things can and should be streamlined in the corporate world, and this book barely scratches the surface.

Andreas Wieman is a Customer Experience (CX) strategist who partners with senior CX leaders to grow their professional brands & drive the best customer experiences.

After spending over 20+ years leading strong operational & support teams for several Fortune 500 clients, Andreas knows what truly drives highly engaged leaders, teams & customers, coupled with the highest standards in process/regulatory adherence, safety, security and fraud prevention practices – and it's not mastering the CX flavor of month.

It's focusing on humanizing each & every interaction, internally & with customers, by delivering solutions driven by technology, talent & vision based on real world practice.

Made in the USA
Columbia, SC
28 June 2024

37856730R00176